CODEPENDENCE
THE DANCE
of WOUNDED
SOULS

A Cosmic Perspective
of Codependence and the
Human Condition

ROBERT BURNEY

Joy to You & Me Enterprises
Cambria, Californ

Although this book makes reference to Alcoholics Anonymous, the principles and Twelve Step program of A.A., this does not mean that A.A. has reviewed or approved the contents of this publication, nor that A.A. agrees with the views expressed herein. A.A. is a program of recovery from alcoholism only—use of this material in connection with programs and activities which are patterned after A.A., but address other problems, or in any other non-A.A. context, does not imply otherwise.

Grateful acknowledgement is made for permission to quote from the following material:

Medicine Cards, by Jamie Sams and David Carson, Copyright 1988, Bear & Co. Reprinted by permission of Bear & Co, P.O. Box 2860, Santa Fe, NM 87504.

Bradshaw On Homecoming "Reclaiming and Championing your Inner Child," a PBS series by John Bradshaw. Reprinted by permission of John Bradshaw, 2412 South Boulevard, Houston TX 77098.

The Book of Runes by Ralph Blum, Copyright 1982, 1987 by Ralph Blum. Reprinted by permission of St. Martin's Press, Inc., New York, NY.

Illusions "The Adventures of a Reluctant Messiah" by Richard Bach. Copyright 1977 by Creature Enterprises, Inc. Reprinted by permission of Bantam Doubleday Dell, New York, N.Y.

Beyond The Quantam by Michael Talbot, Copyright 1986 by Michael Talbot. Reprinted by permission of Simon & Schuster, New York, NY.

ISBN 0-9648383-1-1

Published by
Joy to You & Me Enterprises
Post Office Box 977
Cambria, California 93428

First Edition
Printed in the United States of America
10 9 8 7 6 5 4 3 2 1

*There is a principle which is a bar
against all information, which is proof
against all arguments, and which cannot fail
to keep a man in everlasting ignorance—
that principle is contempt prior to investigation.*

—HERBERT SPENCER

*You can't depend on your eyes
when your imagination is out of focus.*

—MARK TWAIN

Imagination is more important than knowledge.

—ALBERT EINSTEIN

This book is dedicated to:
the wounded souls, the wounded children, in all of us.

ACKNOWLEDGEMENTS

The author extends grateful acknowledgement to the following
people who were messengers and teachers at vitally important
times in the evolution of this book:

Claudia Black—
for being real, for being a friend, for being an angel on my path.

Marianne Duncan—
for the reminder that I am a Spiritual Being
meant to sing a song of Joy.

Jana Cunningham—
for having the openness and willingness to be
the messenger of a most vital message.

Lou Catchings—
for pushing, encouraging, and planting the self-publishing seed.

Jane Vaughan—
for being there when I very much needed a friend, as were Viki
Carlson, Derek Gordon, Terri Roehm & Louie Bennington.

With special thanks to those teachers and messengers of
Truth whose courage and willingness have been such a
shining Light in the darkness, especially

Richard Bach, Melody Beattie, & John Bradshaw.
And to *Betty Ford* for bringing Alcoholism out of the closet.

And to the people who have touched my life
and helped me grow, including
Eleanor Blake, Jessica Stacy, Cynthia Shelton, Deirdre Dunn,
Robert Lugbauer, Scott Mason, Becka Morgan, Steve Gressler,
Carol Ann Arrents, Julie the family therapist, Bobbie Empey,
Cynthia Burr, Jane Duff, Delia Marsellos, Lee Ryan, Ann Lee,
Marty Coffee, Dr. George Henderson, Mary Beth Rossiter,
Sally Burns, Brandi Wood, Francis Wise, Lance Yellowhand
and many others.

*And to my Father and Mother for being absolutely
the best parents they knew how to be.*

CONTENTS

AUTHOR'S FOREWORD

When I first came into contact with the word "Codependent" over a decade ago, I did not think that the word had anything to do with me personally. At that time I heard the word used only in reference to someone who was involved with an Alcoholic—and since I was a Recovering Alcoholic, I obviously could not be Codependent.

I paid only slightly more attention to the Adult Children of Alcoholics Syndrome, not because it applied to me personally—I was not from an Alcoholic family—but because many people whom I knew obviously fit the symptoms of that syndrome. It never occurred to me to wonder if the Adult Child Syndrome and Codependence were related.

As my Recovery from Alcoholism progressed, however, I began to realize that just being clean and sober was not enough. I started to look for some other answers. By that time the conception of the Adult Child Syndrome had expanded beyond just pertaining to Alcoholic families. I started to realize that, although my family of origin had not been Alcoholic, it had indeed been dysfunctional.

I had gone to work in the Alcoholism Recovery field by this time and was confronted daily with the symptoms of Codependence and Adult Child Syndrome. I recognized that the definition of Codependence was also expanding. As I continued my personal Recovery, and continued to be involved in helping others with their Recovery, I was constantly looking for new information. In reading the latest books and attending workshops, I could see a pattern emerging in the expansion of the terms "Codependent" and "Adult Child." I realized that these terms were describing the same phenomenon.

I was troubled, however, by the fact that every book I read, and every expert with whom I came into contact defined "Codependence" differently. I began to try to discover, for my own personal benefit, one all-encompassing definition.

This search led me to examine the phenomenon in an increasingly larger context. I began to look at the dysfunctional nature of society, and then expanded farther into looking at other societies. And finally to the human condition itself. The result of that examination is this book: *Codependence / The Dance of Wounded Souls,* A Cosmic Perspective of Codependence and the Human Condition.

This book is based upon a talk that I have been giving for the last few years. I have edited and reorganized, expanded, added, and clarified information in adapting the talk to book form, but there is still the flavor and style of a talk throughout much of this book. I have not attempted to change this for several reasons, the main reason being that it *works* in conveying the multi-leveled message that I wish to communicate.

One of the reasons for the human dilemma, for the confusion that humans have felt about the meaning and purpose of life, is that more than one level of reality comes into play in the experience of being human. Trying to apply the Truth of one level to the experience of another has caused humans to become very confused and twisted in our perspective of the human experience. It is kind of like the difference between playing the one-dimensional chess that we are familiar with, and the three-dimensional chess played by the characters of Star Trek—they are two completely different games.

That is the human dilemma—we have been playing the game with the wrong set of rules. With rules that do not work. With rules that are dysfunctional.

I was terrified beyond description the first time I gave this talk in June of 1991. It seemed as if emotional memories of what it felt like to be stoned to death by an angry mob were assaulting my being. I went ahead with it anyway, because it is what I needed to do for myself. I needed to stand up in public and own my Truth. I needed to own the Truth that I had come to believe in, the Truth that worked for me to allow me to find some happiness, peace, and Joy in my life. I found that other people found Joy and peace in my message also.

So now I share this message with you, the reader of this book, in the hopes that it will help you to remember the Truth of who you are, and why you are here. This information is not meant to be absolute or the final word—it is meant as an alternative perspective for you to consider. A Cosmic Perspective that just might help to make life an easier, more enjoyable experience for you.

CHAPTER ONE
CODEPENDENCE

A *Transformational Healing Process* has begun on the planet Earth. Due to a profound change that has taken place in the energy field of Collective Human Emotional Consciousness, resources are now available to us to do healing that has *never* before been possible in recorded human history. Human beings now, for the first time, have the capacity to directly address the core issues of the human dilemma.

In order to share with you a Cosmic Perspective of the human condition, to explore the core issues of the human dilemma, and to explain the change that has occurred in planetary conditions, I am going to begin by discussing Truth with a capital "T".

Truth

Truth, in my understanding, is not an intellectual concept. I believe that Truth is an emotional-energy, vibrational communication to my consciousness, to my soul/spirit—my being, from my Soul. Truth is an emotion, something that I feel within.

It is that feeling within when someone says, or writes, or sings, something in just the right words so that I suddenly feel a deeper understanding. It is that "AHA" feeling. The feeling of a light bulb going on in my head. That "Oh, I get it!" feeling. The intuitive feeling when something just feels right ... or wrong. It's that gut feeling, the feeling in my heart. It is the feeling of something resonating within me. The feel-

9

10

ing of remembering something that I had forgotten—but do not remember ever knowing.

In this dance of life that we are doing there are different levels—even of Truth with a capital T. There are ultimate Truths, and there are relative Truths. The ultimate Truths have to do with the eternal, everlasting reality of the God-Force, the Great Spirit. The relative Truths have to do with each individual's own intuitive guidance. These are the messages we receive individually to get us from point A to point B on our individual paths. The guidance we get from our Souls that tells us what the next thing in front of us is.

Our individual, relative Truths expand and grow as we expand and grow. We each have our own unique path to follow—our own individual inner guidance system. *No one can tell you what your path is!* Your Truth is a personal thing. Only you can know your Truth.

It is through following and being True to our individual Truths, as they relate to our path through this physical experience, that we reach balance and harmony with the ultimate Truths.

I am sharing my Truth with you here. I am sharing my heart and my Soul. I ask you, if you can, to be aware of the emotional messages coming from your heart and your Soul as you read this.

For All My Relations

I share my Truth and myself, as a Joyous expression of my Spiritual Being, because it is what I need to do for me. Giving and receiving is what keeps the healing energy flowing for me. I have learned that through giving of what I have received I am healing me.

This is my way of standing up for my Truth, and of honoring "All My Relations," which is a Native American term that refers to the Great Spirit whose essence is present in everyone and everything. We are all related to everyone and everything.

I do this in honor and service to my belief that the ultimate, eternal, blessed Truth is that we are all ONE. That we are all perfect parts of the ONENESS of ALL THAT IS—which is the Universal Creative God-Force.

I share as an expression of Love, as an act of Karmic settlement, and with hope that sharing the Joy that I have found in my Truth will remind you of the Truth which exists within you. Of the Truth of who you Truly are, and why you are here.

Spiritual Beings

The Truth as I feel and understand it is that who we are, are *Spiritual Beings having a human experience*. We are not here as some kind of punishment! We are here to experience being human. To go through that puzzling human experience we call life. The dance of life. The dance that is life.

The Dance of Wounded Souls.

We are the wounded souls. We are the Spiritual Beings who have been wounded by coming into human bodies in the Spiritually-hostile environment that has been present on planet Earth for thousands of years.

The conditions on the planet have changed! That is the Joyous news that I have to share with you. The dance is changing. Since before the dawn of recorded history, the dance of life for humans has been primarily one of survival, of endurance, of suffering.

We have now entered a very special time in human history. An *Age of Healing and Joy* has dawned in human consciousness on this planet. We now have tools, knowledge, and most importantly, clearer access to healing energy and Spiritual guidance than has ever before been available in recorded human history on this planet.

11

12

The dance is changing. A Transformational Healing Process has begun on planet Earth. We have begun the process of breaking out of the vicious, self-perpetuating cycles of destructive behavior that humans have been trapped in for thousands of years. The destructive dance is changing into a dance of healing.

The new dance of healing is most simply called "Recovery," while the old destructive dance has acquired a new name: Codependence.

Codependence

Actually the term "Codependence" is an inaccurate and somewhat misleading term for the phenomenon it has come to describe. A more accurate term would be something like outer-dependence, or external dependence. But it is in the evolution of the understanding of what has come to be called "Codependence" that we have discovered and brought together the tools and knowledge which are so vital to the healing process that has begun. The term has exploded into public consciousness in this society in just the last few years because of the Truth contained within its message.

It is very important to understand that the definition of Codependence has changed radically in recent years. Codependence is a term which has evolved and expanded dynamically since it was first coined. The understanding of Codependence presented here is the next step—a small leap forward—in the natural evolution of the term. A kind of a fast-forwarding in the expanding evolutionary path of the term.

So I am going to discuss the evolution of the term in order to clear up any misunderstandings having to do with out of-date-definitions, such as the one that is being added to dictionaries that are being published now.

Milestones

Before I do that, however, I am going to digress for a moment in order to make a point about this process in which we are involved.

We are involved in a process, a journey, on multiple levels. One level is, of course, the individual level. Another much higher level is the level of the Collective Human Soul: the ONE Soul of which we are all extensions, of which we are all manifestations. We are all experiencing a Spiritual evolutionary process which is unfolding perfectly and always has been.

Everything is unfolding perfectly according to Divine plan, in alignment with precise, mathematically, musically attuned laws of energy interaction.

Both the individual process and the larger human process are marked by milestones. These milestones feel like endings and beginnings, in many instances they feel like and appear to humans to be tragedy. They are in Truth a perfectly planned series of lessons. A perfect part of the unfolding of the Divine script. These milestones are benchmarks in the progress of the process. They mark the beginnings of new phases, new stages.

I bring the term "milestone" up at this point because the term "Codependent" has evolved out of a vitally important event or milestone in this century. A milestone whose ripple effect has been vitally important in laying the groundwork for the change that has taken place in human consciousness.

I believe that in a hundred years historians will look back and pinpoint this milestone as the single most important event in the twentieth century. This milestone was the founding of Alcoholics Anonymous in Akron, Ohio, in June of 1935.

Spiritual Revolution

Besides the invaluable gift of sobriety that AA has given to millions of Alcoholics, it also started a revolution in Spiritual consciousness.

The dramatic success and expansion of AA facilitated the spread of a radically revolutionary idea which has traditionally, in Western Civilization, been considered heresy. This was not a new idea but rather a reintroduction and clarification of an old idea, coupled with a formula for practical application of the concept into day-to-day human life experience.

This revolutionary idea was that an unconditionally Loving Higher Power exists with whom the individual being can personally communicate. A Higher Power that is so powerful that it has no need to judge the humans it created because this Universal Force is powerful enough to ensure that everything unfolds perfectly from a Cosmic Perspective.

This reintroduction of the revolutionary concept of an accessible Loving God has been clarified to specifically include the concept that the individual being can define this Universal Force according to his/her own understanding, and can develop a personal, intimate relationship with this Higher Power.

In other words, no one is needed as an intermediary between you and your creator. No outside agency has the right to impose upon you its definition of God.

The spread of Alcoholics Anonymous, and the other Anonymous programs which sprang out of AA, is the widest and most effective dissemination of this radical revolutionary concept that has ever occurred in Western Civilization.

Mystics, gnostics, and certain "primitive" peoples have, throughout recorded human history, understood the Truth in this concept—but the "organized religions" of urban-based civilizations have persecuted, tortured, and crucified any messengers or groups of people who believed in a Loving, personal God or Goddess—because it threatened the power of those organized religions' control over the masses and therefore their very existence. This time the dissemination of the message has been effective because: The time was right; the revolutionary concept was camouflaged as part of a successful treatment for a fatal, incurable disease; and it was accompanied by the Twelve Step Spiritual program.

The Twelve Step program of AA provides a practical program for accessing Spiritual power in dealing with day-to-day human life. A formula for integrating the Spiritual into the physical. Even though some of the steps, as originally written, contain shaming and abusive wording, the Twelve Step process and the ancient Spiritual principles underlining it are invaluable tools in helping the individual being start down, and stay on, a path aligned with Truth.

It is out of the Twelve Step Recovery movement that our understanding of the dysfunctional nature of civilization has evolved. It is out of the Alcoholic Recovery movement that the term "Codependent" has emerged.

The Evolution of the Term

The phenomenal growth of AA and the success of the disease concept in the treatment of Alcoholism generated the founding of treatment centers in the late 1950s and early 1960s. These early treatment centers were based on what had been successful in early AA. They focused on getting the Alcoholic sober and paid very little attention to the families of Alcoholics.

As these treatment centers matured and evolved, they noticed that the families of Alcoholics seemed to have certain characteristics and patterns of behavior in common. So they started to pay some attention to the families.

A term was coined to describe the significant others of

Alcoholics. That term was "co-alcoholic"—literally "alcoholic with."

The belief was that while the Alcoholic was addicted to alcohol, the co-alcoholic was addicted in certain ways to the Alcoholic. The belief was that the families of Alcoholics became sick because of the Alcoholic's drinking and behavior.

With the drug explosion of the sixties, Alcoholism treatment centers became chemical dependency treatment centers. Co-alcoholics became co-dependents. The meaning was still a literal "dependent with," and the philosophy was much the same.

In the mid-to-late seventies, however, certain pioneers in the field began to look more closely at the behavior patterns of families affected by addiction. Some researchers focused primarily on Alcoholic families, and then graduated to studying adults who had grown up in Alcoholic families. Other researchers started looking more closely at the phenomenon of Family Systems Dynamics.

Out of these studies came the defining of the Adult Child Syndrome, at first primarily in terms of Adult Children of Alcoholics and then expanding to other types of dysfunctional families.

Ironically this research was in a sense a rediscovery of the insight which in many ways was the birth of modern psychology. Sigmund Freud made his early fame as a teenager with his insight into the importance of early childhood trauma. (This was many years before he started shooting cocaine and decided that sex was the root of all psychology.)

What the researchers were beginning to understand was how profoundly the emotional trauma of early childhood affects a person as an adult. They realized that if not healed, these early childhood emotional wounds, and the subconscious attitudes adopted because of them, would dictate the adult's reaction to, and path through, life. Thus we walk around looking like and trying to act like adults, while reacting to life out of the emotional wounds and attitudes of childhood. We keep repeating the patterns of abandonment, abuse, and deprivation that we experienced in childhood.

Psychoanalysis addressed these issues only on the intellectual level—not on the emotional healing level. As a result, a person could go to psychoanalysis weekly for twenty years and still be repeating the same behavior patterns.

As the Adult Child movement, the Family Systems Dynamics research, and the newly emerging "inner child" healing movement expanded and developed in the eighties, the term "Codependent" expanded. It became a term used as a description of certain types of behavior patterns. These were basically identified as "people-pleasing" behaviors. By the middle to late eighties the term "Codependent" was associated with people-pleasers who set themselves up to be victims and rescuers.

In other words, it was recognized that the Codependent was not sick because of the Alcoholic but rather was attracted to the Alcoholic because of his/her disease, because of her/his early childhood experience.

At that time Codependence was basically defined as a passive behavioral defense system, and its opposite, or aggressive counterpart was described as counterdependent. Then most Alcoholics and addicts were thought to be counterdependent.

The word changed and evolved further after the start of the modern Codependence movement in Arizona in the mid-eighties. Co-Dependents Anonymous had its first meeting in October of 1986, and books on Codependence as a disease in and of itself started appearing at about the same time. These Codependence books were the next generation evolved from the books on the Adult Child Syndrome of the early eighties.

17

The expanded usage of the term "Codependent" now includes counterdependent behavior. We have come to understand that both the passive and the aggressive behavioral defense systems are reactions to the same kinds of childhood trauma, to the same kinds of emotional wounds. The Family Systems Dynamics research shows that within the family system, children adopt certain roles according to their family dynamics. Some of these roles are more passive, some are more aggressive, because in the competition for attention and validation within a family system the children must adopt different types of behaviors in order to feel like an individual.

A large part of what we identify as our personality is in fact a distorted view of who we really are due to the type of behavioral defenses we adopted to fit the role or roles we were forced to assume according to the dynamics of our family system.

Behavioral Defenses

I am now going to share with you some new descriptions that I came up with in regard to these behavioral defenses. We adopt different degrees and combinations of these various types of behavior as our personal defense system, and we swing from one extreme to the other within our own personal spectrum. I am going to share these with you because I find them enlightening and amusing—and to make a point.

The Aggressive-Aggressive defense, is what I call the "militant bulldozer." This person, basically the counterdependent, is the one whose attitude is "I don't care what anyone thinks." This is someone who will run you down and then tell you that you deserved it. This is the "survival of the fittest," hard-driving capitalist, self-righteous religious fanatic, who feels superior to most everyone else in the world. This type of person despises the human "weakness" in others because he/she is so terrified and ashamed of her/his own humanity.

The Aggressive-Passive person, or "self-sacrificing bulldozer," will run you down and then tell you that they did it for your own good and that it hurt them more than it did you. These are the types of people who aggressively try to control you "for your own good"—because they think that they know what is "right" and what you "should" do and they feel obligated to inform you. This person is constantly setting him/herself up to be the perpetrator because other people do not do things the "right" way, that is, his/her way.

The Passive-Aggressive, or "militant martyr," is the person who smiles sweetly while cutting you to pieces emotionally with her/his innocent sounding, double-edged sword of a tongue. These people try to control you "for your own good" but do it in more covert, passive-aggressive ways. They "only want the best for you," and sabotage you every chance they get. They see themselves as wonderful people who are continually and unfairly being victimized by ungrateful loved ones—and this victimization is their main topic of conversation/focus in life because they are so self-absorbed that they are almost incapable of hearing what other people are saying.

The Passive-Passive, or "self-sacrificing martyr," is the person who spends so much time and energy demeaning him/herself, and projecting the image that he/she is emotionally fragile, that anyone who even thinks of getting mad at this person feels guilty. They have incredibly accurate, long-range, stealth guilt torpedoes that are effective even long after their death. Guilt is to the self-sacrificing martyr what stink is to a skunk: the primary defense.

These are all defense systems adopted out of a necessity to survive. They are all defensive disguises whose purpose is to protect the wounded, terrified child within.

19

These are broad general categories, and individually we can combine various degrees and combinations of these types of behavioral defenses in order to protect ourselves.

In this society, in a general sense, the men have been traditionally taught to be primarily aggressive, the "John Wayne" syndrome, while women have been taught to be self-sacrificing and passive. But that is a generalization; it is entirely possible that you came from a home where your mother was John Wayne and your father was the self-sacrificing martyr.

Dysfunctional Culture

The point that I am making is that our understanding of Codependence has evolved to realizing that this is not just about *some* dysfunctional families—our very role models, our prototypes, are dysfunctional.

Our traditional cultural concepts of what a man is, of what a woman is, are twisted, distorted, almost comically bloated stereotypes of what masculine and feminine really are. A vital part of this healing process is finding some balance in our relationship with the masculine and feminine energy within us, and achieving some balance in our relationships with the masculine and feminine energy all around us. We cannot do that if we have twisted, distorted beliefs about the nature of masculine and feminine.

When the role model of what a man is does not allow a man to cry or express fear; when the role model for what a woman is does not allow a woman to be angry or aggressive—that is emotional dishonesty. When the standards of a society deny the full range of the emotional spectrum and label certain emotions as negative—that is not only emotionally dishonest, it creates emotional disease.

If a culture is based on emotional dishonesty, with role models that are dishonest emotionally, then that culture is also emotionally dysfunctional, because the people of that society are set up to be emotionally dishonest and dysfunctional in getting their emotional needs met.

What we traditionally have called normal parenting in this society is abusive because it is emotionally dishonest. Children learn who they are as emotional beings from the role modeling of their parents. "Do as I say—not as I do," does not work with children. Emotionally dishonest parents cannot be emotionally healthy role models, and cannot provide healthy parenting.

Our model for what a family should be sets up abusive, emotionally dishonest dynamics.

Consider a scenario where mother is crying in her bedroom and her three year old toddles into the room. To the child it looks as if mom is dying. The child is terrified and says, "I love you mommy!" Mom looks at her child. Her eyes fill with love, and her face breaks into a smile. She says, "Oh honey, I love you so much. You are my wonderful little boy/girl. Come here and give mommy a hug. You make mommy feel so good."

A touching scene? No. Emotional abuse! The child has just received the message that he/she has the power to save mommy's life. That the child has power over, and therefore responsibility for, mommy's feelings. This is emotional abuse, and sets up an emotionally incestuous relationship in which the child feels responsible for the parent's emotional needs.

A healthy parent would explain to the child that it is all right for mommy to cry, that it is healthy and good for people to cry when they feel sad or hurt. An emotionally healthy parent would "role model" for the child that it is okay to have the full range of emotions, all the feelings—sadness and hurt, anger and fear, Joy and happiness, etc.

The Human Condition

Where the Codependence movement has evolved to now, what you'll find the leading figures talking about in their latest books, is cultural Codependence.

The next step which I am proposing in the evolution of the term is to the level of Codependence of civilization.

Codependence as the human condition!

The Codependence Recovery movement is not a fad! It is not a band-aid. It is not a quick fix. It is not "pop" psychology!

Codependence deals with the core issues of the human dilemma.

Codependence has grown out of the cause from which all symptoms arise. That cause is Spiritual dis-ease—not being at ease, at one with Spiritual Self. Not being able to be in balance, in harmony with the universe. All other diseases—physical, emotional, mental—spring out of, are caused by, Spiritual dis-ease.

(The condition of Spiritual dis-ease has been a part of the human experience for so long—for thousands of years— that some of its symptomatic defenses have been genetically adapted by the evolving human species. Alcoholism, I believe, is just one example of a genetically transmitted, physical disease that is an adapted behavioral defense against the pain of Spiritual dis-ease.)

The human condition is a symptom! Human nature as we understand it is a symptom! The human condition is not a result of flaws in human nature. Both are effects.

The condition of Codependence—which, as I said could more accurately be described as outer or external dependence—*is the human condition as we have inherited it!*

CHAPTER TWO
THE DANCE
OF WOUNDED SOULS

The dance of wounded souls is a self-perpetuating cycle of cause and effect that has evolved into becoming the human condition. That dance of Codependence—as it can now be called—is both a cause, a tune that we have been dancing to, and the effect, the dance itself. Codependence is not the original cause—it is a cause in the self-perpetuating cycles of cause and effect that have dictated the course of human evolution.

The original wound, which I will discuss a little later, had the effect of creating a Spiritually hostile condition on this planet. That Spiritually hostile condition then became a cause with many consequences.

Emotions

One of the most devastating of these consequences, or effects, was that human beings began to express emotions in destructive ways. Because the channel between Spiritual Self and human self was disrupted by planetary condition, the human ego began to develop the belief that it was separate from other humans and from the Source. This belief in separation made violence possible.

The violence, caused by the false belief, meant that humans could no longer enjoy a free-flowing emotional process. As a consequence, emotionally-repressive environments evolved in the social systems on this planet. Human beings were forced to adopt defense systems that included

23

24 the belief that emotions were negative and had to be sup-pressed and controlled. This was necessary in order for human beings to live together in communities that would in-sure the survival of the human race.

It is not necessary any longer! And it is dysfunctional.

The act of suppressing emotions was always dysfunc-tional in its effect on the emotional, mental, and Spiritual health of the *individual* being. It was only functional in terms of physical survival of the species.

We now have clearer access to Spiritual healing energy and guidance which allows us to become aligned with Truth so that emotions will not be expressed in destructive ways. We have the tools, knowledge, and guidance to allow emo-tional healing to take place, to allow the individual to enjoy the flow of healthy emotional process.

Attempting to suppress emotions is dysfunctional; it does not work. Emotions are energy: E-motion = energy in motion. It is supposed to be in motion, it was meant to flow.

Emotions have a purpose, a very good reason to be— even those emotions that feel uncomfortable. Fear is a warn-ing, anger is for protection, tears are for cleansing and releas-ing. These are not negative emotional responses! We were taught to react negatively to them. It is our reaction that is dysfunctional and negative, not the emotion.

Emotional honesty is absolutely vital to the health of the being. Denying, distorting, and blocking our emotions in reaction to false beliefs and dishonest attitudes causes emo-tional and mental disease. This emotional and mental dis-ease causes physical, biological imbalance which produces physical disease.

Codependence is a deadly and fatal disease because of emotional dishonesty and suppression. It breaks our hearts, scrambles our minds, and eventually kills our physical body vehicles because of the Spiritual dis-ease, because of our wounded souls.

The key to healing our wounded souls is to get clear and honest in our emotional process. Until we can get clear and honest with our human emotional responses—until we change the twisted, distorted, negative perspectives and reactions to our human emotions that are a result of having been born into, and grown up in, a dysfunctional, emotionally repressive, Spiritually hostile environment—we cannot get clearly in touch with the level of emotional energy that is Truth. We cannot get clearly in touch with and reconnected to our Spiritual Self.

We, each and every one of us, has an inner channel to Truth, an inner channel to the Great Spirit. But that inner channel is blocked up with repressed emotional energy, and with twisted, distorted attitudes and false beliefs.

We can intellectually throw out false beliefs. We can intellectually remember and embrace the Truth of ONENESS and Light and Love. But we cannot integrate Spiritual Truths into our day-to-day human existence, in a way which allows us to substantially change the dysfunctional behavior patterns that we had to adopt to survive, until we deal with our emotional wounds. Until we deal with the subconscious emotional programming from our childhoods.

We cannot learn to Love without honoring our Rage!

We cannot allow ourselves to be Truly Intimate with ourselves or anyone else without owning our Grief.

We cannot clearly reconnect with the Light unless we are willing to own and honor our experience of the Darkness.

We cannot fully feel the Joy unless we are willing to feel the Sadness.

We need to do our emotional healing, to heal our wounded souls, in order to reconnect with our Souls on the highest vibrational levels. In order to reconnect with the God-Force that is Love and Light, Joy and Truth.

E - Motion

Emotional energy is not only supposed to be in motion, to flow, it is also the energy that gets us in motion. It is what drives us, what propels us forward through life. When emotional flow is blocked and suppressed it does not go away. Energy cannot simply disappear. It can transform but it cannot disappear. That is a law of physics.

Emotional energy that is suppressed still drives us. It is what causes obsessive-compulsive behavior, it is what drives addictions. Repressed emotional energy builds up pressure that has to be released. It has to manifest somehow, some way. It has to transform into some kind of manifestation.

This is true in any human system. It is true for the individual being, in family systems, in communities, in societies.

Repressed emotions drive us to workaholism, to compulsive exercise, to religious addiction, to self-righteous and self-destructive obsessions. Trying to keep those emotions repressed causes us to use substances like alcohol and drugs, food and cigarettes, to keep stuffing it down, to keep sucking it back in.

Repressed emotions explode outward in violence and war, in carnage and rape. We are raping the planet we live on, we are raping ourselves. Any emotional explosion outward in an act of violence is an act of violence against Self.

Repressed emotions implode, explode inward to cause the system to become dysfunctional. In the individual being this manifests as disease—emotional, mental, and physical disease. In larger systems, in families, in societies, that dysfunction manifests as child abuse and incest, as crime and poverty, homelessness and pollution.

The dance that we learn as children—the repression and distortion of our emotional process in reaction to the attitudes and behavior patterns we adopt to survive in an emotionally repressive, Spiritually hostile environment—is the dance we keep dancing as adults.

We are driven by repressed emotional energy. We live life in reaction to childhood emotional wounds. We keep trying to get the healthy attention and affection, the healthy love and nurturing, the being-enhancing validation and respect and affirmation, that we did not get as children.

This dysfunctional dance is Codependence. It is Adult Child Syndrome. It is the tune that humans have been dancing to for thousands of years. Vicious, self-perpetuating cycles of self-destructive behavior.

The original wound created a condition that caused the Spiritual dis-ease, the Spiritual disconnection. That in turn caused the emotional repression—the damming, the blocking of the emotional process which perpetuated the cycles.

Human beings are not damned with an n. We are emotionally dammed. Dammed up, blocked up—which is what causes us to feel damned with an n.

Inner Children

We are set up to be emotionally dysfunctional by our role models, both parental and societal. We are taught to repress and distort our emotional process. We are trained to be emotionally dishonest when we are children.

This emotional repression and dishonesty causes society to be emotionally dysfunctional. Additionally, urban-based civilization has completely disregarded natural laws and natural cycles such as the human developmental process. There is no integration into our culture of the natural human developmental process.

As just one blatant example of this, consider how most so called primitive or aboriginal societies react to the onset of puberty. When a girl starts menstruating, ceremonies are held to celebrate her womanhood—to honor her coming into her power, to honor her miraculous gift of being able to conceive.

27

Boys go through training and initiation rites to help them make the transition from boyhood into manhood. Look at what we have in our society: junior high school—a bunch of scared, insecure kids who torture each other out of their confusion and fear, and join gangs to try to find an identity.

This lack of integration of the natural human growth process causes trauma. At each stage of the developmental process we were traumatized because of the emotionally repressive, Spiritually hostile environment into which we were born. We went into the next stage incomplete and then were retraumatized, were wounded again.

We have a feeling place (stored emotional energy), and an arrested ego-state within us for an age that relates to each of those developmental stages. Sometimes we react out of our three-year-old, sometimes out of our fifteen-year-old, sometimes out of the seven-year-old that we were.

If you are in a relationship, check it out the next time you have a fight: Maybe you are both coming out of your twelve-year-olds. If you are a parent, maybe the reason you have a problem sometimes is because you are reacting to your six-year-old child out of the six-year-old child within you. If you have a problem with romantic relationships maybe it is because your fifteen-year-old is picking your mates for you.

The next time something does not go the way you wanted it to, or just when you are feeling low, ask yourself how old you are feeling. What you might find is that you are feeling like a bad little girl, a bad little boy, and that you must have done something wrong because it feels like you are being punished.

Just because it feels like you are being punished does not mean that is the Truth. *Feelings are real*—they are emotional energy that is manifested in our body—*but they are not necessarily fact.*

What we feel is our "emotional truth" and it does not necessarily have anything to do with either facts or the emotional energy that is Truth with a capital "T"—especially when we our reacting out of an age of our inner child.

If we are reacting out of what our emotional truth was when we were five or nine or fourteen, then we are not capable of responding appropriately to what is happening in the moment; we are not being in the now.

When we are reacting out of old tapes based on attitudes and beliefs that are false or distorted, then our feelings cannot be trusted.

When we are reacting out of our childhood emotional wounds, then what we are feeling may have very little to do with the situation we are in or with the people with whom we are dealing in the moment.

In order to start *be*-ing in the moment in a healthy, age-appropriate way it is necessary to heal our "inner child." The inner child we need to heal is actually our "inner children" who have been running our lives because we have been unconsciously reacting to life out of the emotional wounds and attitudes, the old tapes, of our childhoods.

Grieving

The way to stop reacting out of our inner children is to release the stored emotional energy from our childhoods by doing the grief work that will heal our wounds. The only effective, long term way to clear our emotional process—to clear the inner channel to Truth which exists in all of us—is to grieve the wounds which we suffered as children. The most important single tool, the tool which is vital to changing behavior patterns and attitudes in this healing transformation, is the grief process. The process of grieving.

We are all carrying around repressed pain, terror, shame, and rage energy from our childhoods, whether it was twenty

29

years ago or fifty years ago. We have this grief energy within us even if we came from a relatively healthy family, because this society is emotionally dishonest and dysfunctional.

When someone "pushes your buttons," he/she is activating that stored, pressurized grief energy. She/he is gouging the old wounds, and all of the newer wounds that are piled on top of those original wounds by our repeating behavior patterns.

We are terrified of this pressurized pain, terror, shame, and rage energy—of "having our buttons pushed"—because we have experienced it in the past as instances where we have explosively overreacted in ways that caused us to later feel ashamed and crazy, or as implosive reactions that have thrown us into that deep dark pit of emotional despair within.

We are walking around with this set of buttons available to be pushed by any person, place, thing, or combination thereof that recreates the dynamics of the situation wherein we were originally wounded. (For example: a certain smell, the texture of a fabric, a tone of voice, a gesture, etc., can be emotional triggers that throw us back to an age of our inner child.)

We carry this set of buttons, this baggage, with us until we release that stored, pressurized grief energy in a healthy grieving process. This society's answer to behavior caused by unresolved grief is to shame you, label you, lock you up, and/or give you drugs. We do not have to play that game anymore. We have new tools now, and we have rediscovered the healing power of the natural grieving process.

It is through healing our inner child, our inner children, by grieving the wounds that we suffered, that we can change our behavior patterns and clear our emotional process. We can release the grief with its pent-up rage, shame, terror, and pain from those feeling places which exist within us.

That does not mean that the wound will ever be completely healed. There will always be a tender spot, a painful place within us due to the experiences that we have had. What it does mean is that we can take the power away from those wounds. By bringing them out of the darkness into the Light, by releasing the energy, we can heal them enough so that they do not have the power to dictate how we live our lives today. We can heal them enough to change the quality of our lives dramatically. We can heal them enough to Truly be happy, Joyous and free in the moment most of the time.

It is through having the courage and willingness to revisit the emotional "dark night of the soul" that was our childhood, that we can start to understand on a gut level why we have lived our lives as we have.

Forgiveness

It is when we start understanding the cause and effect relationship between what happened to the child that we were, and the effect it had on the adult we became, that we can Truly start to forgive ourselves. It is only when we start understanding on an emotional level, on a gut level, that we were powerless to do anything any differently than we did that we can Truly start to Love ourselves.

The hardest thing for any of us to do is to have compassion for ourselves. As children we felt responsible for the things that happened to us. We blamed ourselves for the things that were done to us and for the deprivations we suffered. There is nothing more powerful in this transformational process than being able to go back to that child who still exists within us and say, "It wasn't your fault. You didn't do anything wrong, you were just a little kid."

To be able to say "I Love you" to the child/children within us, and to the person who we are today, and really mean it on an emotional level, is one of the goals of this process.

Until we can forgive ourselves and Love ourselves we

32 cannot Truly Love and forgive any other human beings—including our parents who were only doing the best they knew how. They, too, were powerless to do anything any different—they were just reacting to their wounds.

It is necessary to own and honor the child who we were in order to Love the person we are. And the only way to do that is to own that child's experiences, honor that child's feelings, and release the emotional grief energy that we are still carrying around.

Honoring the Feelings

This grieving is not an intellectual process. Changing our false and dysfunctional attitudes is vital to the process; enlarging our intellectual perspective is absolutely necessary to the process, but doing these things does not release the energy—it does not heal the wounds.

Learning what healthy behavior is will allow us to be healthier in the relationships that do not mean much to us; intellectually knowing Spiritual Truth will allow us to be more Loving some of the time; but in the relationships that mean the most to us, with the people we care the most about, when our "buttons are pushed" we will watch ourselves saying things we don't want to say and reacting in ways that we don't want to react—because we are powerless to change the behavior patterns without dealing with the emotional wounds.

We cannot integrate Spiritual Truth or intellectual knowledge of healthy behavior into our experience of life in a substantial way without honoring and respecting the emotions. We cannot consistently incorporate healthy behavior into day to day life without being emotionally honest with ourselves. We cannot get rid of our shame and overcome our fear of emotional intimacy without going through the feelings.

Walking around saying "We are all one," and "God is Love," and "I forgive them all," does not release the energy. Using crystals, or white light, or being born again does not heal the wounds, and does not fundamentally alter the behaviors.

We are all ONE and God is LOVE; crystals do have power and white light is a very valuable tool, but we need to not confuse the intellectual with the emotional (forgiving someone intellectually does not make the energy of anger and pain disappear)—and to not kid ourselves that using the tools allows us to avoid the process.

There is no quick fix! Understanding the process does not replace going through it! There is no magic pill, there is no magic book, there is no guru or channeled entity that can make it possible to avoid the journey within, the journey through the feelings.

No one outside of Self (True, Spiritual Self) is going to magically heal us.

There is not going to be some alien E.T. landing in a spaceship singing, "Turn on your heart light," who is going to magically heal us all.

The only one who can turn on your heart light is you.

The only one who can give your inner children healthy parenting is you.

The only healer who can heal you is within you.

Discernment

Now we all need help along the way. We all need guidance and support. And it is a vitally important part of the healing process to learn to ask for help.

It is also a vital part of the process to learn discernment. To learn to ask for help and guidance from people who are trustworthy, people who will not betray, abandon, shame, and abuse you. That means friends who will not abuse and betray you. That means counselors and therapists who will not judge and shame you and project their issues onto you.

[I believe that the cases of "false memories" that are getting a lot of publicity these days are in reality cases of emotional incest—which is rampant in our society and can be devastating to a person's relationship with his/her own sexuality—that are being misunderstood and misdiagnosed as sexual abuse by therapists who have not done their own emotional healing and project their own issues of emotional incest and/or sexual abuse onto their patients.]

Someone who has not done her/his own emotionally healing grief work cannot guide you through yours. Or as John Bradshaw put it in his excellent PBS series on reclaiming the inner child, "No one can lead you somewhere that they haven't been."

Learning discernment is vital—not just in terms of the choices we make about who to trust, but also in terms of our perspective, our attitudes.

We learned about life as children and it is necessary to change the way we intellectually view life in order to stop being the victim of the old tapes. By looking at, becoming conscious of, our attitudes, definitions, and perspectives, we can start discerning what works for us and what does not work. We can then start making choices about whether our intellectual view of life is serving us—or if it is setting us up to be victims because we are expecting life to be something which it is not.

One of the core characteristics of this disease of Codependence is intellectual polarization—black and white thinking. Rigid extremes—good or bad, right or wrong, love it or leave it, one or ten. Codependence does not allow any gray area—only black and white extremes.

Life is not black and white. Life involves the interplay of black and white. In other words, the gray area is where life takes place. A big part of the healing process is learning the numbers two through nine—recognizing that life is not black and white.

Life is not some kind of test, that if we fail, we will be punished. We are not human creatures who are being punished by an avenging god. We are not trapped in some kind of tragic place out of which we have to earn our way by doing the "right" things.

We are Spiritual Beings having a human experience. We are here to learn. We are here to go through this process that is life. We are here to feel these feelings.

Doing our emotional healing allows us to feel clear about what is in front of us instead of torturing ourselves by obsessively thinking, trying to figure out what's right and what's wrong.

The Truth is that the intellectual value systems, the attitudes, that we use in deciding what's right and wrong were not ours in the first place. We accepted on a subconscious and emotional level the values that were imposed on us as children. Even if we throw out those attitudes and beliefs intellectually as adults, they still dictate our emotional reactions. Even if, especially if, we live our lives rebelling against them. By going to either extreme—accepting them without question or rejecting them without consideration—we are giving power away.

In order to stop giving our power away, to stop reacting out of our inner children, to stop setting ourselves up to be victims, so that we can start learning to trust and Love ourselves, we need to begin to practice discernment.

Discernment is having the eyes to see, and the ears to hear—and the ability to feel the emotional energy that is Truth.

We cannot become clear on what we are seeing or hearing if we are reacting to emotional wounds that we have not been willing/able to feel and subconscious attitudes that we have not been willing/able to look at.

We cannot learn to trust ourselves as long as we are still setting ourselves up to be victimized by untrustworthy people. We cannot learn to Love ourselves enough to meet our own needs until we start to release the attitudes and feelings that tell us that we are unworthy—that it is somehow shameful to be ourselves. We cannot learn to Love ourselves without learning discernment.

The black and white thinking of Codependence causes us to either keep the baby in the dirty bath water or throw out both. Discernment is picking the baby out of the dirty bath water.

We can learn to trust and Love ourselves through learning to make healthier choices about who to trust and what to believe. We can begin to be able to recognize Truth and throw out the distortions, false beliefs, and lies. By doing our emotional healing, by changing the dysfunctional attitudes, we can start being responsible in our lives—that is, we can begin to have the ability to respond to life honestly in the moment.

Until we heal our wounds, until we become honest and clear in our emotional process, we are not able to be discerning. We are not capable of responding to life in the now—we are only able to react out of old grief, out of old tapes.

Trust

As long as we are reacting out of old grief and old tapes then our feelings cannot be trusted to give us accurate information. There is an exception to this: In life and death situations or in a big crisis, we can sometimes access intuitive Truth directly. Which is a reason that many of us put ourselves in a lot of those kind of situations—or create crises for ourselves. That is one time when we can trust ourselves.

Recovery is a process of learning to trust ourselves.

Codependence is based upon not trusting ourselves.

The way the emotional defense system that is Codependence works is that we continue to repeat our patterns in order to reinforce the belief that it is not safe to trust. Not safe to trust ourselves or this process we call life.

Codependence does this to protect us. Because it was not safe for us to trust our own feelings, senses, and perceptions as children our egos decided that it is never safe to trust.

Codependence is an emotional and behavioral defense system which was adopted by our egos in order to meet our need to survive as a child. Because we had no tools for reprogramming our egos and healing our emotional wounds (culturally approved grieving, training and initiation rites, healthy role models, etc.), the effect is that as an adult we keep reacting to the programming of our childhood and do not get our needs met—our emotional, mental, Spiritual, or physical needs. Codependence allows us to survive physically but causes us to feel empty and dead inside. Codependence is a defense system that causes us to wound ourselves.

Some people, when they first get into Recovery, when they first start on a healing path, mistakenly believe that they are supposed to take down their defenses and learn to trust everyone. That is a very dysfunctional belief. It is necessary to take down the dysfunctional defense systems but we have to replace them with defenses that work. We have to have a defense system, we have to be able to protect ourselves. There is still a hostile environment out there full of wounded Adult Children whom it is not safe to trust.

In our disease defense system we build up huge walls to protect ourselves and then—as soon as we meet someone who will help us to repeat our patterns of abuse, abandonment, betrayal, and/or deprivation—we lower the drawbridge and invite them in. We, in our Codependence, have radar systems which cause us to be attracted to, and attract to us, the people, who for us personally, are exactly the most untrustworthy (or unavailable or smothering or abusive or whatever we need to repeat our patterns) individuals—exactly the ones who will "push our buttons."

This happens because those people feel familiar. Unfortunately in childhood the people whom we trusted the most—were the most familiar—hurt us the most. So the effect is that we keep repeating our patterns and being given the reminder that it is not safe to trust ourselves or other people.

Once we begin healing we can see that the Truth is that it is not safe to trust as long as we are reacting out of the emotional wounds and attitudes of our childhoods. Once we start Recovering, then we can begin to see that on a Spiritual level these repeating behavior patterns are opportunities to heal the childhood wounds.

The process of Recovery teaches us how to take down the walls and protect ourselves in healthy ways—by learning what healthy boundaries are, how to set them, and how to defend them. It teaches us to be discerning in our choices, to ask for what we need, and to be assertive and Loving in meeting our own needs. (Of course many of us have to first get used to the revolutionary idea that it is all right for us to have needs.)

Recovery involves bringing to consciousness those beliefs and attitudes in our subconscious that are causing our dysfunctional reactions so that we can reprogram our ego defenses to allow us to live a healthy, fulfilling life instead of just surviving. So that we can own our power to make choices for ourselves about our beliefs and values instead of unconsciously reacting to the old tapes. Recovery is consciousness raising. It is en-light-en-ment—bringing the dysfunctional attitudes and beliefs out of the darkness of our subconscious into the Light of consciousness.

On an emotional level the dance of Recovery is owning

and honoring the emotional wounds so that we can release the grief energy—the pain, rage, terror, and shame that is driving us.

That shame is toxic and is not ours—it never was! We did nothing to be ashamed of—we were just little kids. Just as our parents were little kids when they were wounded and shamed, and their parents before them, etc., etc. This is shame *about being human* that has been passed down from generation to generation.

There is no blame here, there are no bad guys, only wounded souls and broken hearts and scrambled minds.

Because of our broken hearts, our emotional wounds, and our scrambled minds, our subconscious programming, what the disease of Codependence causes us to do is abandon ourselves. It causes the abandonment of self, the abandonment of our own inner child—and that inner child is the gateway to our channel to the Higher Self.

The one who betrayed us and abandoned and abused us the most was ourselves. That is how the emotional defense system that is Codependence works.

The battle cry of Codependence is *"I'll show you—I'll get me."*

The War Within

The dysfunctional dance of Codependence is caused by being at war with ourselves—being at war within.

We are at war with ourselves because we are judging and shaming ourselves for being human. We are at war with ourselves because we are carrying around suppressed grief energy that we are terrified of feeling. We are at war within because we are "damming" our own emotional process—because we were forced to become emotionally dishonest as children and had to learn ways to block and distort our emotional energy.

39

We cannot learn to Love ourselves and be at peace within until we stop judging and shaming ourselves for being human and stop fighting our own emotional process, until we stop waging war on ourselves.

In a war, soldiers are forced to deny their emotions in order to survive. This emotional denial works to help the soldier survive the war, but later can have devastating delayed consequences. The medical profession has now recognized the trauma and damage that this emotional denial can cause, and have coined a term to describe the effects of this type of denial. That term is "Delayed Stress Syndrome."

In a war soldiers have to deny what it feels like to see friends killed and maimed; what it feels like to kill other human beings and have them attempting to kill you. There is trauma caused by the events themselves. There is trauma due to the necessity of denying the emotional impact of the events. There is trauma from the effects the emotional denial has on the person's life after he/she has returned from the war—because as long as the person is denying his/her emotional trauma she/he is denying a part of her/himself.

The stress caused by the trauma, and the effect of denying the trauma, by denying self, eventually surfaces in ways which produce new trauma—anxiety, alcohol and drug abuse, nightmares, uncontrollable rage, inability to maintain relationships, inability to hold jobs, suicide, etc.

Codependence is a form of Delayed Stress Syndrome.

Instead of blood and death (although some do experience blood and death literally), what happened to us as children was spiritual death and emotional maiming, mental torture and physical violation. We were forced to grow up denying the reality of what was happening in our homes. We were forced to deny our feelings about what we were experiencing and seeing and sensing. We were forced to deny our selves.

We grew up having to deny the emotional reality: of parental alcoholism, addiction, mental illness, rage, violence, depression, abandonment, betrayal, deprivation, neglect, incest, etc. etc.; of our parents fighting or the underlying tension and anger because they weren't being honest enough to fight; of dad's ignoring us because of his workaholism and/or mom smothering us because she had no other identity than being a mother; of the abuse that one parent heaped on another who wouldn't defend him/herself and/or the abuse we received from one of our parents while the other wouldn't defend us; of having only one parent or of having two parents who stayed together and shouldn't have; etc., etc.

We grew up with messages like: children should be seen and not heard; big boys don't cry and little ladies don't get angry; it is not okay to be angry at someone you love—especially your parents; god loves you but will send you to burn in hell forever if you touch your shameful private parts; don't make noise or run or in any way be a normal child; do not make mistakes or do anything wrong; etc., etc.

We were born into the middle of a war where our sense of self was battered and fractured and broken into pieces. We grew up in the middle of battlefields where our beings were discounted, our perceptions invalidated, and our feelings ignored and nullified.

The war we were born into, the battlefield each of us grew up in, was not in some foreign country against some identified "enemy"—*it was in the "homes" which were supposed to be our safe haven with our parents whom we Loved and trusted to take care of us.* It was not for a year or two or three—*it was for sixteen or seventeen or eighteen years.*

We experienced what is called "sanctuary trauma"— our safest place to be was not safe—and we experienced it on a daily basis for years and years. Some of the greatest damage was done to us in subtle ways on a daily basis because our sanctuary was a battlefield.

It was not a battlefield because our parents were wrong or bad—it was a battlefield because they were at war within, because they were born into the middle of a war. By doing our healing we are becoming the emotionally honest role models that our parents never had the chance to be. Through being in Recovery we are helping to break the cycles of self-destructive behavior that have dictated human existence for thousands of years.

Codependence is a very vicious and powerful form of Delayed Stress Syndrome. The trauma of feeling like we were not safe in our own homes makes it very difficult to feel like we are safe anywhere. Feeling like we were not lovable to our own parents makes it very difficult to believe that anyone can Love us.

Codependence is being at war with ourselves—which makes it impossible to trust and Love ourselves. Codependence is denying parts of ourselves so that we do not know who we are.

Recovery from the disease of Codependence involves stopping the war within so that we can get in touch with our True Self, so that we can start to Love and trust ourselves.

Perspective

In order to find out who we are, we have to start being emotionally honest with ourselves. And in order to be emotionally honest with ourselves, we have to start changing our perspective on our own emotional process.

As a child, I learned from the role modeling of my father that the only emotion that a man felt was anger. From my mother, whose definition of love included the belief that you cannot be angry at someone you love, I learned that it was not okay to be angry at anyone I loved. That left me with very little permission to feel anything. That did not mean that I did not have feelings—it meant that I was at war with my own emotions, that I could not be honest with myself about having them. As long as I could not be honest with myself emotionally there was no way I could know who I was. Until I started owning the grief and rage from my childhood, the sadness and hurt and fear that I had denied all of my life, I was incapable of being honest with myself, incapable of knowing who I Truly was.

It was impossible to start Loving myself and trusting myself, impossible to start finding some peace within, until I started to change my perspective of, and my definitions of, who I was and what emotions it was okay for me to feel.

Enlarging my perspective means changing my definitions, the definitions that were imposed on me as a child about who I am and how to do this life business. In Recovery it has been necessary to change my definitions of, and my perspective of, almost everything. That was the only way that it was possible to start learning how to Love myself.

I spent most of my life feeling like I was being punished because I was taught that God was punishing and that I was unworthy and deserved to be punished. I had thrown out those beliefs about God and life on a conscious, intellectual level in my late teens—but in Recovery I was horrified to discover that I was still reacting to life emotionally based on those beliefs.

I realized that my perspective of life was being determined by beliefs that I had been taught as a child even though they were not what I believed as an adult. That perspective caused my emotional truth to be that I felt like life was punishing me, and that I was not good enough—that something was wrong with me. I felt like a victim of life, like a victim of myself, at the same time that I was blaming others for not making me happy.

I had to start trying to find a concept of a Higher Power

44 who could Love me even though I was an imperfect human. If my Creator is judging me then who am I not to judge myself? On the other hand if the Goddess Loves me unconditionally then who am I not to Love myself? And if the God/Goddess/Great Spirit/Universal Force Truly Loves me then everything has to be happening for reasons that are ultimately Loving.

The more I came to believe and trust—what some place deep inside of me I could feel, could remember, was the Truth—that all of the pieces of this puzzle of life fit together perfectly, and that there are no accidents, no coincidences, no mistakes, the more I was able to accept and Love myself and others. And the more I was able to trust the process, myself, and my Higher Power.

I learned that even though there are things that *feel* like mistakes, that even though life sometimes *feels* like punishment, that those feelings are not the Truth. I learned that my emotional truth was being dictated by my subconscious perspectives of life, by the definitions of life that had been imposed on me as a child, by the subconscious attitudes that I had adopted because of the emotional traumas I had experienced as a child.

Perspective is a key to Recovery. I had to change and enlarge my perspectives of myself and my own emotions, of other people, of God and of this life business. Our perspective of life dictates our relationship with life. We have a dysfunctional relationship with life because we were taught to have a dysfunctional perspective of this life business, dysfunctional definitions of who we are and why we are here.

It is kind of like the old joke about three blind men describing an elephant by touch. Each one of them is telling his own Truth, they just have a lousy perspective. Codependence is all about having a lousy relationship with life, with being human, because we have a lousy perspective on life as a human.

The only way that I was able to make significant progress in the process of stopping self-judgment and getting rid of the toxic shame was to become conscious of the larger perspective. When I started to believe that maybe a Higher Power, a Universal Force, existed which was Truly All-Powerful and Unconditionally Loving then life started to become a lot easier and more enjoyable. Then I could start to see that the "accidents" and "coincidences" are really miracles. That the "mistakes" are really opportunities for growth.

Faith

I do not believe that it is possible for any human being to fully understand how it all works, for anyone to see the whole puzzle. What we can do though is to start having some faith, start remembering (what I am doing here is reminding you of what you already know on some level) that all of the pieces do fit together perfectly, that everything is unfolding perfectly according to the Divine purpose of a Loving Universal Force—and that we are Spiritual Beings who are a perfect part of that Force who have come to Earth to have this human experience.

We need to be willing to start having some faith. We need to be willing to start changing our perspectives. We need to be willing to start feeling the feelings. We need to be willing to start remembering Truth.

There is Truth all around us. We can find messages everywhere once we start picking the baby out of the bathwater—once we begin to be willing and open to feeling and trusting the emotional energy communications of Truth from our Souls. The teachings of all of the Master Teachers, of all religions, philosophies, mythologies, fairy tales, even comic books, have Truth in them.

Once I began to become conscious of the emotional

45

messages I was getting from my body instead of just trying to figure things out in my head, then I had a choice to follow the guidance I was receiving. I could let my gut reaction choose the books I read. I could let my heart guide me to the talks or workshops that I needed to attend. I realized that if my attention was drawn to something—an author, a workshop, a certain type of healing therapy, a psychic, a gathering, a movie, anything that caught my attention on a feeling level—three or more times from different sources in a short time span that the Universe was probably sending me a message.

When I was willing to hear and see the messages—and take action based upon them—I began to discover the Truth around me. There were certain books of Truth that I was led to that were especially important in my consciousness raising, in my Recovery process. I am now going to quote a story from one of those books which means a lot to me. It is a story from a book called *Medicine Cards* by Jamie Sams and David Carson. This book deals with the Medicine Wheel, and the totem animals of the Medicine Wheel Spiritual beliefs of certain Native American tribes.

The subject of this particular story is the Swan totem—Swan power:

As Swan looked high above Sacred Mountain, she saw the biggest swirling black hole she had ever seen. Dragonfly came flying by, and Swan stopped him to ask about the black hole. Dragonfly said, "Swan, that is the doorway to the other planes of imagination. I have been guardian of the illusion for many, many moons. If you want to enter there, you would have to ask permission and *earn* the right."

Swan was not so sure that she wanted to enter the black hole, She asked Dragonfly what was necessary for her to earn entry. Dragonfly replied, "You must be willing to accept whatever the future holds as it is presented, without trying to change the Great Spirit's plan." Swan looked at her ugly little duckling body and then answered, "I will be happy to abide by Great Spirit's plan. I won't fight the currents of the black hole. I will *surrender* to the flow of the spiral and *trust* what I am shown." Dragonfly was very happy with Swan's answer and began to spin the magic to break the pond's illusion. Suddenly, Swan was engulfed by a whirlpool in the center of the pond.

Swan reappeared many days later, but now she was graceful and white and long-necked. Dragonfly was stunned! "Swan what happened to you!'" he exclaimed. Swan smiled and said, "Dragonfly, I learned to surrender my body to the power of Great Spirit and was taken to where the future lives. I saw many wonders high on Sacred Mountain and because of my faith and my acceptance I have been changed. I have learned to accept a state of Grace."

A "state of Grace" is the condition of being Loved unconditionally by our Creator *without having to earn that Love.* We are Loved unconditionally by the Great Spirit. What we need to do is *to learn to accept* that state of Grace.

The way we do that is to change the attitudes and beliefs within us that tell us that we are not Lovable. And we cannot do that without going through the black hole. The black hole that we need to surrender to traveling through is the black hole of our grief. The journey within—through our feelings—is the journey to knowing that we are Loved, that we are Lovable.

It is through willingness and acceptance, through surrender, trust, and faith, that we can begin to own the state of Grace which is our True condition.

We are all beautiful swans who exist in a state of Grace,

48 in a condition of being unconditionally Loved. The dance of Recovery is a process of learning to accept and integrate the Truth of Grace into our lives.

The goal in this Age of Healing and Joy is integration and balance. To integrate the Spiritual Truth into our physical experience so that we can fill the hole inside and find wholeness within. As we integrate our True Spiritual nature into our relationship with our physical being we can begin to achieve some balance and harmony with and between all of the parts of our being.

This age is a time for growing and learning, a time to become conscious of the True nature of the Source Energy, a time of Spiritual Awakening. We have been given the wonder-full gift of having the ability and the tools to start integrating the Truth of a Loving Universal Force into our day-to-day experience of life. We now have the knowledge and guidance that we need to start bringing some balance to our relationships—with ourselves and our God/Goddess, with other people and the planet—so that we can live in a way that allows us to experience some Peace and Love on our life path.

We can heal our wounded souls enough to change the dance of life from a dance of endurance and suffering to a dance that celebrates living. We now have access to the power to transform the dance of Codependence to a dance of healing and Joy.

CHAPTER THREE
THE HUMAN
CONDITION

This dance of Codependence is a dance of dysfunctional relationships—of relationships that do not work to meet our needs. That does not mean just romantic relationships, or family relationships, or even human relationships in general.

The fact that dysfunction exists in our romantic, family, and human relationships is a *symptom* of the dysfunction that exists in our relationship with life—with being human. It is a symptom of the dysfunction which exists in our relationships with ourselves as human beings.

And the dysfunction that exists in our relationship with ourselves is a symptom of Spiritual dis-ease, of not being in balance and harmony with the universe, of feeling disconnected from our Spiritual source.

That is why it is so important to enlarge our perspective. To look beyond the romantic relationship in which we are having problems. To look beyond the dysfunction that exists in our relationships with other people.

The more we enlarge our perspective, the closer we get to the cause instead of just dealing with the symptoms. For example, the more we look at the dysfunction in our relationship with ourselves as human beings the more we can understand the dysfunction in our romantic relationships.

As was stated earlier, our perspective of life dictates our relationship with life. This is true for all types of relationships. Our perspective of God dictates our relationship with God. Our perspective of what a man or a woman is, dictates

49

our relationship with ourselves as men or women, and with other men and women. Our perspective of our emotions dictates our relationship with our own emotional process.

Changing our perspectives is absolutely vital to the growth process. And the process of enlarging our perspective can sometimes convert that which seems to be very complex and totally beyond our understanding into something that is simple and understandable.

Simple Formula

What I am going to share with you now is a simple formula that I believe helps to explain this incredibly complex phenomena. It is simple, elementary, fundamental, and the cause of the human condition as I understand it.

The cause of Codependence, the cause of the dysfunction that exists in the human experience, is that humans (due to certain planetary conditions which will be discussed later) have been perceiving, and doing, "human" *backwards*. We have been *reversed* in our perspective and in our interactive dynamics—our relationship—with this human life experience. The world is a mess today because we have been perceiving this human business backwards.

This "reversity" begins with the basic premise of who we are as beings. We are not weak, sinful, shameful human creatures who have to somehow earn the right to become Spiritual. We are Spiritual Beings having a human experience. That is a 180-degree swing in perspective. It changes everything!

As John Lennon said, "Imagine." Imagine a world based upon this knowledge.

The belief that there is something inherently wrong or shameful about being human is all-pervasive in human civilized society. It is woven into the fabric of civilized societies around the world.

There is nothing shameful or bad about being human!

We are NOT being punished for something some dude did in a Garden thousands of years ago!!!

We are NOT being punished because some angels tried a coup d'etat on some bearded male god!

We are NOT being punished, as some of the new age psychics and channeled entities claim, as the result of our ancestors becoming trapped in the lower vibrational frequencies because they liked sex too much, or procreated with animals.

THAT IS ALL BULLSHIT!!!

Those are twisted, distorted, grotesquely warped misinterpretations of what were originally symbolic, metaphoric, allegorical attempts to explain the unexplainable. They no longer contain more than an echo of a grain of Truth in them. They have been distorted so grotesquely because of the shame which humans assumed came with the pain of the original wound.

We are also not trapped in a vale of tears because there is no God-Force. We do not exist simply because of some biological accident.

And we are not going through a cycle of lifetimes simply because that is all there is—or as Buddha supposedly taught, of which the goal is to cease to exist.

I say supposedly because it is very difficult to discern what Buddha actually taught and what distortions polluted the Truth which he accessed.

The teachings of all the Master Teachers, of all the world's religions, contain some Truth along with a lot of distortions and lies. Discerning Truth is often like recovering treasure from shipwrecks that have been sitting on the ocean floor for hundreds of years—the grains of Truth, the nuggets of gold, have become encrusted with garbage over the years.

The Bible

As one example of this, I am going to discuss the Bible for a moment, because it has been such a powerful force in shaping the attitudes of Western Civilization.

The Bible contains Truth, much of it symbolic or in parable form because most of the audience at the time it was written had very little sophistication or imagination. They did not have the tools and the knowledge we have access to now.

So the Bible does contain Truth—it also contains a lot of distortion. The Bible was translated many times. *It was translated by male Codependents.*

I am going to share with you a short excerpt from a recently published book. I have not read this book and cannot tell you much about it. I have read a review of this book which appeared in *California* magazine in November of 1990. What I am sharing here is from that review.

I offer this to you: Not to say that this new translation of the Bible is right and the old one is wrong—it is for you to decide which one *feels more like Truth* to you. I offer this as I offer everything else that I am sharing here—as an alternate perspective for you to consider.

This book is called *The Book of J.* It was written by two men—one of whom is a former head of the Jewish Publication Society, the other is a professor of humanities at Yale University. What they have done in this book is to extract what they believe is one voice from the Old Testament. The Old Testament is a compilation of writings by many different writers. That is why there are two conflicting versions of the Creation in Genesis because it was written by two different people.

They have taken the voice of one of those writers, gone back as far as they could to the original language, and translated it from a different perspective.

Here is a short excerpt from the Old Testament as an

example of the difference between their translation and the traditional version. The traditional version is taken from the King James Bible, Genesis 3:16. It says: "And thy desire shall be to thy husband, and he shall rule over thee."

Sounds like the normal patriarchal, sexist tone in which we have always accepted that the Bible was written.

Here is the new translation of the exact same phrase: "To your man's body your belly will rise, for he shall be eager above you."

Now to me, "rule over you" and "eager above you" mean two very different things—it actually seems pretty close to being a 180 degree swing in perspective. This new translation sounds as if there is nothing shameful about sex. As if maybe it is not bad to have a normal human sex drive, maybe it is not True that the flesh is weak and the spirit exists somewhere way out there.

The reviewer (Greil Marcus, *California* magazine, November 1990, Vol. 15, No.11), without ever quite perceiving the shame connection, says that this book "...is an act of violence...to what we think we know." He says that, "...it's a great change, in the way one sees the human condition." He also states that, "The differences...are many and profound..." and include "...*the replacement of 'man became a living soul' with 'man becomes a creature of flesh'—without the distinction between soul and flesh, Christianity, or, as Michael Ventura calls it, Christianism, dissolves.*"

This retranslation shows that basic misconception and misunderstanding may be at the heart, at the foundation of Western Civilization, or to quote the reviewer, "In other words, the argument is that within Jewish, Christian, and Islamic civilization, certainly within Western Civilization, at its heart—or at its foundation—is a ruin."

What he could not quite put his finger on as the act of violence against the very core of Jewish, Christian, and

54   Islamic civilization is that what this book seems to do is to take the shame out of being human—of being creatures of flesh. There is no shame in being human. We are not being punished by God. It just *feels* like it sometimes.

Buddha

Now to get back to Buddha. We are told—by writers who wrote all of it down long after he was dead, of course—that Buddha taught that there were four Great Truths. (This is one interpretation of Buddha's teachings which is being used here as a tool. It is not meant to diminish or negatively reflect on the Spiritual value of other versions.)

The first was that all existence is suffering.

That is not True! It has never been True!

As I stated earlier, life for humans has been primarily about suffering. But there have always been moments of transcendence. Moments of Joy and Light and Love in human life. Moments of connecting with the Truth and Joy of our Spiritual Essence. Moments of connection with the Great Spirit.

If there had not been, human life would be without real meaning, and we probably would have given up the fight for survival long ago.

We are not animals—not that there is anything wrong with being an animal—but we have a consciousness of something larger, something beyond ourselves. We have a memory of some other place—of some place kinder and gentler and more Loving.

We are Spiritual Beings.

Humans have always searched for our Spiritual connection. Every human who has ever lived on this planet has ached for, yearned for, Spiritual full-fill-ment. Every human (who is not in denial) feels the hole inside that comes from Spiritual dis-ease, from feeling disconnected from our Spiritual Source.

What is so wonderful, what is so Joyous and exciting, is that we now have clearer access to our Spiritual Higher Consciousness than ever before in recorded human history. And through that Higher Self to the Universal Creative God-Force.

Each and every one of us has an inner channel. We now have the capability to *atone*—which means *tune into*—to atone, to tune into the Higher Consciousness. To tune into the Higher vibrational emotional energies that are Joy, Light, Truth, Beauty, and Love.

We can tune into the Truth of "at ONE ness." Atone = at ONE. Atonement = at ONE ment, in a condition of ONENESS.

We now have access to the highest vibrational frequencies—we can tune into the Truth of ONENESS. By aligning with Truth we are tuning into the higher energy vibrations that reconnect us with the Truth of ONENESS.

This is the age of atonement, but it does not have anything to do with judgment and punishment. It has to do with tuning our inner channel into the right frequencies.

But our inner channel is blocked and cluttered with repressed emotional energy and dysfunctional attitudes. The more we clear our inner channel through aligning with Truth attitudinally, and releasing the repressed emotional energy through the grief process, the clearer we can tune into the music of Love and Joy, Light and Truth.

It is not easy because we have been taught to look at being human backwards. We were forced to accept a reversed perspective. We were emotionally and subconsciously programmed to react to life dysfunctionally based on reversed belief systems.

We are Spiritual Beings having a human experience.

NOT human creatures who have to earn Spiritual existence. We are not flawed, shameful humans who have to do human perfectly, who have to do the "right" things in order

55

56 to transcend.

Buddha—who was obviously an important messenger in setting up this defense system—taught that the fourth great truth is that one must control conduct, thinking, and belief by following the eight-fold path of right views, right speech, right conduct, right effort, right etc., etc.

Buddha could have been the patron saint of Codependence with that teaching. Always trying to be in control and do the "right" things is Codependence (as is going to the opposite extreme). It is a defense system for survival in a hostile environment. It is based on beliefs that are backwards, reversed.

Who we are, are transcendent Spiritual Beings who are part of the ONENESS that is the God-Force. We always have been and always will be. We are perfect in our Spiritual Essence. We are perfectly where we are supposed to be on our Spiritual Path. And from a human perspective we will never be able to do "human" perfectly—which is perfect.

We have been trying to do "human" perfectly according to a false belief system in order to "get Spiritual." It does not work. It's dysfunctional and backwards. It is not bad or wrong or shameful—it is the best we have known how to do life until now.

All any human being in the history of the planet has ever done is the best that she/he knew how to do to survive in the moment.

Humans have always been looking for a way home. For a way to connect with our Higher Consciousness. For a way to reconnect with our creator. Throughout human history, human beings have used temporary artificial means to raise their vibrational frequency, to try to reconnect with Higher Consciousness.

Drugs and alcohol, meditation and exercise, sex and religion, starvation and overeating, the self-torture of the flagellant or the deprivation of the hermit—all are attempts to connect with higher consciousness. Attempts to reconnect with Spiritual Self. *Attempts to go home.*

Outer Dependence

Buddha's second great truth is that it is "the craving," the "thirst for life," that causes suffering. That it is our desires and human needs that cause us suffering.

His third great truth is that to stop suffering we must destroy the thirst for life, stamp out the desires and needs.

He lived 2500 years too soon. It is not human needs and desires that cause suffering, it is looking to get those needs fulfilled in someplace where they cannot be fulfilled that causes suffering. It has been trying to quench our thirst from an empty well that is dysfunctional.

Humans have been trying to fill the hole within ourselves by looking outside of ourselves. We were taught to look outside, to external manifestations to meet our needs, to find out who we are and why we are here.

The answers do not exist outside—the answers lie within.

The reason that humans have not been able to "get *it* together" is that we have been looking outside for "it." "It" exists only within. We need to look *in-to-it.* As in intuition: in-tu-it.

As long as we look outside of Self—with a capital S—to find out who we are, to define ourselves and give us self-worth, we are setting ourselves up to be victims.

We were taught to look outside of ourselves—to people, places, and things; to money, property, and prestige—for fulfillment and happiness. It does not work, it is dysfunctional. We cannot fill the hole within with anything outside of Self.

You can get all the money, property, and prestige in the

world, have everyone in the world adore you, but if you are not at peace within, if you don't Love and accept yourself, none of it will work to make you Truly happy.

When we look outside for self-definition and self-worth, we are giving power away and setting ourselves up to be victims. *We are trained to be victims. We are taught to give our power away.*

As just one small example of how pervasively we are trained to be victims, consider how often you have said, or heard someone say, "I have to go to work tomorrow." When we say "I have to" we are making a victim statement. To say, "I have to get up, and I have to go to work," is a lie. No one forces an adult to get up and go to work. The Truth is "I choose to get up and I choose to go to work today, because I choose to avoid the consequences of not working." To say, "I choose," is not only the Truth—it is empowering and acknowledges an act of self-Love. When we "have to" do something we feel like a victim. And because we feel victimized, we will then be angry, and want to punish, whomever we see as forcing us to do something we do not want to do— such as our family, or our boss, or society.

Self-Worth

Not only were we taught to be victims of people, places, and things, we were taught to be victims of ourselves, of our own humanity. We were taught to take our ego-strength, our self-definition from external manifestations of our being.

Our bodies are not who we are—they are a part of our being in this lifetime—but they are not who we Truly are.

Looks deteriorate, talent dissipates, intelligence erodes. If we define ourselves by these external manifestations, then we will be victimized by the power we give them. We will hate ourself for being human and aging.

Looks, talent, intelligence—external manifestations of

our being—are gifts to be celebrated. They are *temporary* gifts. They are not our total being. They do not define us or dictate if we have worth.

We were taught to do it backwards. To take our self-definition and self-worth from temporary illusions outside of, or external to our beings. It does not work. It is dysfunctional.

As was stated earlier, Codependence could more accurately be called outer or external dependence. Outside influences (people, places, and things; money, property, and prestige) or external manifestations (looks, talent, intelligence) can not fill the hole within. They can distract us and make us feel better temporarily but they cannot address the core issue—they cannot fulfill us Spiritually. They can give us ego-strength but they cannot give us self-worth.

True self-worth does not come from temporary conditions. True self-worth comes from accessing the eternal Truth within, from remembering the state of Grace that is our True condition.

No one outside of you can define for you what your Truth is.

Nothing outside of you can bring you True fulfillment. You can only be fully filled by accessing the transcendent Truth that already exists within.

This Age of Healing and Joy is a time for each individual to access the Truth within. It is not a time for gurus or cults or channeled entities, or anyone else, to tell you who you are.

Outside agencies—other people, channeled entities, this book—can only remind you of what you already know on some level.

Accessing your own Truth is remembering.

It is following your own path.

It is finding your bliss.

Codependence does not work. It is dysfunctional. It is backwards.

IN-dependence is the answer.

Looking outside of ourselves for self-definition and self-worth means that we have to judge people in order to feel good about ourselves. There is no other way to do it when you look outside.

We were taught to have ego-strength through judgment—better than, prettier than, smarter than, richer than, stronger than, etc., etc.

In a Codependent society everyone has to have someone to look down on in order to feel positive about him/herself. This is the root of all bigotry, racism, sexism, and prejudice in the world.

True self-worth does not come from looking down on anyone or anything. True self-worth comes from awakening to our connection to everyone and everything.

The Truth is that we are like snowflakes: Each individual is unique and different and special and we are all made from the same thing. We are all cut from the same cloth. We are all part of the Eternal ONENESS that is the Great Spirit.

When we start looking within and celebrating the Truth of who we Truly are, then we can celebrate our unique differences instead of judging them out of fear.

Reversed Perspectives of Life

We were taught to approach life from a perspective of fear, survival, lack and scarcity. The Truth of the Universal Creative Force is *Unconditional Love, Joy, and Abundance.* Again, a 180-degree shift in perspective.

We were taught that life is about destinations, and that when we get to point x—be it marriage or college degree or fame and fortune or whatever—we will live happily ever after.

That is not the way life works. You know that now, and probably threw out that fairy tale ending stuff intellectually a long time ago. But on some emotional level we keep looking for it because that is what the children in us were taught. We keep living life as if it is a dress rehearsal for "when our ship comes in." For when we really start to live. For when we get that relationship, or accomplishment, or money that will make us okay, that will fix us.

We do not need fixing. We are not broken. Our sense of self, our self perception, was shattered and fractured and broken into pieces, not our True Self.

We think and feel like we are broken because we were programmed backwards.

We are not broken. That is what toxic shame is—thinking that we are broken, believing that we are somehow inherently defective.

Guilt is "I made a mistake, I did something wrong."

Shame is "I'm a mistake, something is wrong with me."

Again, the feelings of that little child inside who believes that he/she deserves to be punished.

Life is a journey, a process—it's not a destination. Life is continuous and constant change and growth. We were taught to fight and try to control the change, to resist the growth. We were taught to swim upstream, to go against the flow. No wonder we get tired sometimes.

We were taught that death is a great tragedy and that we should spend our lives fearing and ignoring it. We were taught to fear death and to never live life. That's backwards.

Death is a transition, a transformation, death is a milestone in the longer journey. It is not a tragedy to be feared—it is an eventuality to be accepted. What is tragedy is not enjoying living while we are here.

We have been looking at life, at this human experience, from a reversed perspective.

We were taught a reversed, backwards concept of god. We were taught about a god who is a small, petty, angry, jealous, judgmental, male being. We were taught about a god who is an abusive father.

If you choose to believe in a punishing, judgmental, male god, that is your total right and privilege. If that works for you, great. It does not work for me. I think the concept is reversed.

We were taught to be caretakers instead of care-givers. That is, to take our self-definition—our ego-strength—from what we do for others, rather than giving to others out of our Self as an expression of Love.

This is a matter of focus: Codependence is a disease of reversed focus. If you are taking your self-worth from what you are doing for others, you are going to end up being the victim, because they are not going to do what you want them to do in return. ("After all that I've done for you!")

If you are giving as an expression of self-worth then you do not need anything in return—and that is when you really get the gifts.

Giving should be an expression of the Love we have accessed within—not a way of gaining ego-strength by helping people whom we are judging to be less than us.

We live in a society where a few have billions while others are starving and homeless. We live in a society which believes that it is not only possible to own and hoard the resources and the land but one which can rationalize killing the planet we live on. These are symptoms of imbalance, of reversed thinking.

There is imbalance in all aspects of our society. There are inherent conflicts of interest in the dynamics of our systems.

We live in a society where the medical system profits from disease and does not have any incentive—does not make any profit—for promoting health.

Imagine if you will a system where the healer gets paid every month that you are healthy and does not get paid if you are sick. Do you think doctors would be more open to herbs and acupuncture, holistic healing and nutrition, and other kinds of alternative healing methods? Of course the economy would collapse because the drug and insurance companies would go bankrupt.

There is something backwards about a medical system that needs to cut you open and/or give you drugs to perpetuate itself.

Our mental health system not only does not promote healing—it actually blocks the process. The mental health system in this country is designed to get your behavior and emotions under control so that you can fit back into the dysfunctional system.

Drugs that are designed to disconnect you from your feelings block the healing process. Mental health professionals who need to have you see them regularly in order to be financially supported, need to have you be dependent upon them—need to keep you a patient in order to survive.

We live in a society where sex is somehow shameful and should not be talked about—but we use sex to sell cars. That is backwards. Human sexuality is a blessed gift to be honored and celebrated not twisted and distorted into something demeaning and shameful.

We live in a society where the emotional experience of "love" is conditional on behavior. Where fear, guilt, and shame are used to try to control children's behavior because parents believe that their children's behavior reflects their self-worth.

In other words, if little Johnny is a well-behaved, "good boy," then his parents are good people. If Johnny acts out, and misbehaves, then there is something wrong with his parents. ("He doesn't come from a good family.")

What the family dynamics research shows is that it is actually the good child—the family hero role—who is the most emotionally dishonest and out of touch with him/herself, while the acting-out child—the scapegoat—is the most

63

64 emotionally honest child in the dysfunctional family. Backwards again.

In a Codependent society we are taught, in the name of "love," to try to control those we love, by manipulating and shaming them, to try to get them to do the *right* things—in order to protect our own ego-strength. Our emotional experience of love is of something controlling: "I love you if you do what I want you to do." Our emotional experience of love is of something that is shaming and manipulative and abusive.

Love that is shaming and abusive is an insane, ridiculous concept. Just as insane and ridiculous as the concept of murder and war in the name of God.

These ridiculous, insane, reversed, and dysfunctional concepts are a part of the basis of civilizations on this planet.

Civilized Society

I want to make a couple of points of clarification at this time.

One is that I am referring to civilizations around the world, but most of the examples or specifics I am mentioning have to do with Western Civilization and specifically American society. That is just for my convenience and your identification. (I am using the word "civilization" here in the Western sense of the term—that is, urban-based and believed to be superior to "less advanced" peoples.)

All civilizations are dysfunctional to varying degrees, as are subcultures within those civilizations. They just have different flavors of dysfunction, of imbalance.

As an example: In much of Asia the individual is discounted for the good of the whole—whether that be family or corporation or country. The individual takes his or her self-definition from the larger system. That is just as out of balance and dysfunctional as the Western Civilization manifestation of glorifying the individual to the detriment of the whole. It is just a different variety of dysfunction.

The goal of this dance of Recovery is integration and balance. That means *celebrating being a tree while also glorying in being a part of the forest.* Recovery is a process of becoming conscious of our individual wholeness and our ONENESS with all.

The other point I want to make is that I am saying "civilized" society for a reason. It is in urban-based industrialized civilization that the optimum dysfunction has been manifested in this world.

Many so-called primitive or aboriginal tribal cultures, such as the Native Americans, had far more integrated and balanced cultures for their place and time than any "civilization." They were not totally integrated and balanced by any means. They were, however, closer to the rhythms of nature and had respect for nature and natural laws, so were more aligned with universal laws than urban-based civilizations.

In fact, many of the primitive societies were far more functional in terms of the Spiritual, emotional, and mental health of the *individual* members of the society, and had far more respect for the individual members, than any so-called "civilized" society on this planet.

I believe that historically there has been a direct correlation between the level of advancement—of "progress"—and the level of dysfunction in terms of the individual being's level of fulfillment and happiness. In other words, the more "advanced" the society became (that is, the farther it removed itself from respect for, and alignment with, natural laws and cycles), the more dysfunctional it became in terms of the individual being's feelings of self-respect and fulfillment.

[The historical inverse relationship between progress and individual emotional health was somewhat altered in accordance with the Divine Script so that we could reach this Age of Healing and Joy that we have now entered. This alteration was accomplished through the efforts of a series of mystical messengers who taught the importance of individual rights. These messengers laid the groundwork for a group of mystics, with names like Jefferson and Franklin, to create a society where individuals could pursue Spiritual Truth despite the disapproval of the government and the majority of the society. (Of course, because of the dysfunctional nature of the society, that right was honored in theory rather than practice much of the time—but the right was inherent in the framework of the society.) This inherent right is what made it possible for the United States to became the spawning ground for the Transformational Healing Movement that has begun on the planet. A great acceleration of this process took place with the national trauma/gift that was the sixties and Viet Nam. This period forced individuals to start questioning the traditional value systems, the traditional perspectives, on a massive scale. All of the pieces of the puzzle fit together perfectly when we look at them in a large enough perspective.]

Another reason that some of these so-called "primitive" cultures were more functional is that they also had a much more benevolent idea about a Higher Power. They actually believed that the God-Force had a Loving purpose for putting us here instead of it being some kind of punishment which was shameful.

So the more advanced, the more civilized, a society became, the more dysfunctional it became in terms of serving the emotional, mental, and Spiritual needs of the individual members of the society. Sounds kind of backwards doesn't it?

Heal Your Inner Child

These are some of the backward, reversed aspects of this human condition of Codependence. I believe that this formula works in all areas and that the core causes of any manifestation in the world today can be explained as a rational, logical consequence of this "reversity."

Our society declares war on symptoms instead of healing the cause. We have a war on crime, a war on poverty, a war on drugs (illegal drugs that is). Obviously fighting a war on symptoms does not work—it's backwards, it's dysfunctional.

The wars outside of us are a reflection of the war within. Humans have been at war within and without for thousands of years. The wars, the violence, the rape of mother Earth that is happening, are all caused by the war within being projected outward.

It is all caused by warring on ourselves. By judging and feeling ashamed of ourselves for being human—and by fighting our own emotional process.

The way to stop the war within is through healing and learning to Love our own inner child/children. The inner child is the gateway to discovering our True Self—to reconnecting with the Great Spirit.

I have wanted for years to print a bumper sticker that says: "Work for World Peace - Heal your Inner Child"

Because that is the only way it can be done. That is the only way that will work.

Saddam Hussein was beaten by his stepfather on almost a daily basis—he was emotionally abandoned and shamed by his mother. He is just an Adult Child acting out of his childhood trauma. Because of his broken heart and wounded soul and reversed thinking, he has been trying to prove to himself that he is the biggest kid on the block, and that his parents should not have treated him that way. He has caused hundreds of thousands of people to be killed in the process.

Adolf Hitler killed six million Jews to try to eradicate what he hated about himself: his own Jewish heritage. He was full of shame and had a hole within—a wounded soul. He felt unworthy and unloved and he struck out against that which he, in his reversed, twisted thinking, identified as the cause of his wounds.

67

We cannot stop the wars outside until we stop the war within!

The way to do that is to focus on our own individual healing—to start dancing the dance of Recovery. We have been doing it backwards. We have been trying to fix the external in order to find peace internally.

It does not work. It is dysfunctional.

CHAPTER FOUR
THE DANCE OF RECOVERY

We were taught to look at and do "human" backwards. We need to make a 180-degree swing in our perspectives.

That includes our perspective on this healing process. Many of us have pursued healing and Recovery just like we did the rest of our lives—as if it were a destination to be reached where we would find "happily ever after." We have gone to healers and psychics and therapists in order to learn the "right" way to do life.

Recovery is not a dance of right and wrong, of black and white—it is a dance of integration and balance. The questions in Recovery are: Is it working for you? Is the way you live your life working to meet your needs? Is the way you are living your life bringing you some happiness?

When I state that the grief process works, I am not saying that it is the "right" thing to do, or that you are bad or wrong if you are not actively pursuing your emotional healing.

Maybe it has not been time for you to do your grief work yet. Maybe you have not had a safe place to do it. Maybe it is not part of your path in this lifetime.

No one can tell you what your path is!

What I am telling you is that the grief process *works* to dramatically change the quality of the life experience. What I am saying is that it is possible to find some Peace and Joy in life. Unfortunately, in sharing this information I am forced to use language that is polarized—that is black and white.

When I say that you cannot Truly Love others unless

you Love yourself—that does not mean that you have to completely Love yourself first before you can start to Love others. The way the process works is that every time we learn to Love and accept ourselves a little tiny bit more, we also gain the capacity to Love and accept others a little tiny bit more.

When I say that you cannot start to access intuitive Truth until you clear out your inner channel—I am not saying that you have to complete your healing process before you can start getting messages. You can start getting messages as soon as you are willing to start listening. The more you heal the clearer the messages become.

When I talk about ways that we use to go unconscious—like workaholism, or exercise, or food, or whatever—I am not saying that you should be ashamed if you are doing some of these things.

We cannot go from unconscious to conscious overnight! This healing is a long gradual process. We all still need to go unconscious sometimes. Recovery is a dance that celebrates progress, not one that achieves perfection.

A significant breakthrough in my personal process came when I was able to recognize, and give myself credit for, the progress that I had made—when I realized that a pint of Häagen-dazs was lasting me three days instead of being gone within twenty minutes of when I bought it.

That was a very big breakthrough for me, to be able to give myself credit for the progress instead of judging and shaming myself for not being perfect, for still feeling like I needed the nurturing of ice cream.

We had to learn to go unconscious in order to survive! Thank God for alcohol or television or romance novels. Thank God for ice cream!

We need to stop judging ourselves—that means allowing ourselves to do whatever it takes, whatever works. There are times when we need to go unconscious. There are times when we need to stuff our feelings in the moment. There are times when it is not safe to be vulnerable and emotionally honest.

This Recovery process is a *gradual* transition from using our old tool box to using the new tools. The old tools—the ways we used to go unconscious so we could survive—are not "bad" or "wrong." They were life savers—without them we would be either dead or mass murderers, or dead mass murderers.

We adopted the old tools because they were the best choices that were available to us at the time. We adopted them in response to intuitive impulses that were "right on." Those impulses were "protect myself, nurture myself." It is the nature of the defense system that is Codependence that the ways we learned to protect and nurture ourselves are self-abusive in the long run.

So we need to stop shaming ourselves for the behaviors that we adopted to protect and nurture ourselves, at the same time that we are transitioning to behaviors that are less self-abusive.

Notice that I say *less* self-abusive. We are talking progress, not perfection here.

If you have an image of what completely healthy behavior is, and you will not allow yourself to accept and Love yourself until you get there, then you are setting conditions under which you decide when you will become Lovable. You are still buying into a concept of conditional love and by extension, the concept of a Higher Power that is conditionally loving. You are still trying to earn, and become worthy of not only self-Love, but also God's Love. That small child inside of you is still trying to earn your parents' Love and validation.

That is a natural, normal thing for humans beings on this Codependent planet. Try not to judge and beat yourself up for it. Try to observe it and say, "Oh, isn't it sad that I am

71

still doing that? I think I will try to learn some ways that I can change it."

Enjoying Life

Everything is unfolding perfectly from a Cosmic Perspective!

There are no accidents, no coincidences, no mistakes!

You are perfectly where you are supposed to be on your Path. You always have been and always will be!

The God-Force is powerful enough to get us to where we are supposed to be with or without our help! We do not have the power to screw up the Great Spirit's plan.

What we do have is the option of making it easier on ourselves. *The goal in Recovery is not to become perfect.* The goal is to make life an easier, more enjoyable experience.

The way I think of it is that my Higher Power works with the carrot and stick approach: like a mule driver trying to get a mule moving, he can either dangle a carrot in front of the mule and get the mule moving after the carrot, or he can take a stick and beat him until he gets moving.

It is a lot easier on me to follow the carrots that my Higher Power dangles in front of me than to force the Universe to use a stick to get me moving. Either way I am going to get to where the Universe wants me—but the carrot method is a lot easier on me.

The more that I do my healing, the clearer I get on receiving the messages—the more I get to follow the carrots instead of experiencing the stick. The dance of Recovery is a process of starting to Love ourselves enough to start changing life into an easier, more enjoyable experience.

So what I am saying is not that you are doing something wrong if you are not happy with your life. I am saying, "Hey, this is the reason that doing life the way we were taught doesn't work—it is not our fault!" I am saying, "Hey, there are answers, there is hope. We have new tools now—and they work! Isn't that great news?"

This healing process works. It works miraculously because in aligning with Truth we come into harmony with the universal laws of energy interaction. We learn to go with the natural healthy flow instead of being at war with it. We learn to Love and accept ourselves instead of being at war within.

Butterflies

In order to become aligned with Truth so that we can stop the war within and change life into an easier, more enjoyable experience, it is vitally important to become clear in our emotional process and to change the reversed attitudes that we had to adopt to survive. Those reversed attitudes are what cause our dysfunctional perspectives—which in turn, have caused us to have a lousy relationship with life.

I am going to quote from a book now, and again a little later, that is my own personal favorite book of Truth. I feel a great deal of Truth in this book. It has guided me and helped me to remember my Truth and to become conscious of my path. It was a very important part of my personal process of enlarging my perspective—of being able to see this life business in a larger context.

It is a book called *Illusions* by Richard Bach. This is one of my favorite quotations from that book.

The mark of your ignorance is the depth of your
belief in injustice and tragedy.
What a caterpillar calls the end of the world the
master calls a butterfly.

The "depth of your belief" is about perspective. If we are reacting to life emotionally out of the belief systems we had imposed on us as children we will then see change as tragedy and feel that being forced to grow is shameful. As we

73

74 change our attitudes toward this life experience, when we can start viewing it as a process, a journey, then we can begin to see that what we used to perceive as problems are really opportunities for growth. Then we can begin to realize that even though our experiences in childhood have caused us to think of ourselves as, and feel like, lowly caterpillars—we are in Truth butterflies who are meant to fly.

We are all butterflies. We are all Spiritual Beings.

The Critical Parent/Disease Voice

One of the difficulties in this healing process is that even after we start to awaken to being butterflies, a part of our mind keeps telling us that we are low, crawling, disgusting creatures.

Taking the power away from that part of us is the key to the healing process. A key to stopping the war inside. *We need to take the shame and judgment out of the process on a personal level.* It is vitally important to stop listening and giving power to that critical place within us that tells us that we are bad and wrong and shameful.

That "critical parent" voice in our head is the disease lying to us. Any shaming, judgmental voice inside of us is the disease talking to us—*and it is always lying.* This disease of Codependence is very adaptable, and it attacks us from all sides. The voices of the disease that are totally resistant to becoming involved in healing and Recovery are the same voices that turn right around and tell us, using Spiritual language, that we are not doing Recovery good enough, that we are not doing it right.

We need to become clear internally on what messages are coming from the disease, from the old tapes, and which ones are coming from the True Self—what some people call "the small quiet voice."

We need to turn down the volume on those loud, yammering voices that shame and judge us and turn up the volume on the quiet Loving voice. As long as we are judging and shaming ourselves we are feeding back into the disease, we are feeding the dragon within that is eating the life out of us. Codependence is a disease that feeds on itself—it is self-perpetuating.

This healing is a long gradual process—the goal is progress, not perfection. What we are learning about is unconditional Love. Unconditional Love means no judgment, no shame.

[When I use the term "judge," I am talking about making judgments about our own or other people's beings based on behavior. In other words, I did something bad therefore I am a bad person; I made a mistake therefore I am a mistake. That is what toxic shame is all about: feeling that something is wrong with our being, that we are somehow defective because we have human drives, human weaknesses, human imperfections.

There may be behavior in which we have engaged that we feel ashamed of, but that does not make us shameful beings. We may need to make judgments about whether our behavior is healthy and appropriate but that does not mean that we have to judge our essential self, our being, because of the behavior. Our behavior has been dictated by our disease, by our childhood wounds; it does not mean that we are bad or defective as beings. It means that we are human, it means that we are wounded.

It is important to start setting a boundary between being and behavior. *All humans have equal Divine value as beings*—no matter what our behavior. Our behavior is learned (and/or reactive to physical or physiological conditions). Behavior, and the attitudes that dictate behavior, are adopted defenses designed to allow us to survive in the Spiritually hostile, emotionally repressive, dysfunctional environments into which we were born.]

75

We judge others negatively for being human because we judge ourselves negatively for being human. We cannot Truly Love and accept others unless we start to Love ourselves as beings and accept our humanity.

We need to start *observing* ourselves and stop judging ourselves. Any time we judge and shame ourselves, we are feeding back into the disease, we are jumping back into the squirrel cage.

This is a brilliantly insidious disease!

The war within cannot be won by fighting the disease, by fighting ourselves. The only way to break out is to start giving ourselves a break, to start being kind to, and having compassion for, ourselves and our inner children. We cannot begin to make progress in learning to Love ourselves until we start being kind to ourselves in healthy ways. A very important part of being kind to ourselves is learning how to say no, and how to set, and be able to defend, boundaries.

Unconditional Love does not mean being a doormat for other people—unconditional Love begins with Loving ourselves enough to protect ourselves from the people we Love if that is necessary.

Internal Boundaries

In order to Love ourselves we need to have boundaries within as well as external boundaries. Codependence is a disease of self-victimization—"I'll show you, I'll get me!" We need to stop feeding the dragon within by giving power to the part of us that shames and judges us. We need to stop listening to the disease voices which tell us that we "should" be able to control things over which we have no control.

I spent most of my life doing the Serenity prayer backwards, that is, trying to change the external things over which I had no control—other people and life events mostly—and taking no responsibility (except shaming and blaming myself) for my own internal process—over which I can have some degree of control. Having some control is not a bad thing; trying to control something or somebody over which I have no control is what is dysfunctional. It was very important for me to start learning how to recognize the boundaries of where I ended and other people began, and to start realizing that I can have some control over my internal process in ways that are not shaming and judgmental—that I can stop being the victim of myself.

I spent most of my life being the victim of my own thoughts, my own emotions, my own behaviors. I was consistently picking untrustworthy people to trust and unavailable people to love. I could not trust my own emotions because I was incapable of being honest with myself emotionally—which made me incapable of Truly being honest on any level.

I had to become willing and open and honest enough to start becoming conscious of the dysfunctional attitudes, the dysfunctional perspectives. I had to become willing to learn discernment in order to make choices about the changes I needed to make in my perspectives—especially my perspective on my own emotional process.

Once I started to feel the feelings, to do the grief work, then I could begin to trust myself to be discerning about which of my emotions were telling me the Truth. Only then was I able to substantially change my relationship with my God, with myself, and with life.

I learned that I was able to feel and release the feelings without having them destroy me. I learned that I could change my mental attitudes, I could change the way I think, so that my mind was no longer my worst enemy. I learned that by owning and honoring my inner children and their emotional wounds I was able to take the power away from those wounds—by releasing the stored energy—so that I had choices over how I would respond instead of blindly reacting.

I learned that I could trust myself to have the wisdom to rec-ognize Truth so that I could accept the things that I could not change and change the things I had some control over.

When I became willing to surrender the old attitudes and beliefs, to surrender to feeling the feelings, to surrender trying to control things over which I had no control, then I accessed the power to change myself and my relationships. I became empowered to change my life into an experience that was defined by Joy, Love, and Peace instead of fear, anger, and pain.

It was vitally important for me to learn how to have internal boundaries so that I could lovingly parent (which, of course, includes setting boundaries for) my inner children, tell the critical parent/disease voice to shut up, and start accessing the emotional energy of Truth, Beauty, Joy, Light, and Love. It was by learning internal boundaries that I could begin to achieve some integration and balance in my life, and transform my experience of life into an adventure that is enjoyable and exciting most of the time.

Integrating Truth

One of most important steps to empowerment is inte-grating Spiritual Truth into our experience of the process. In order to do that it is necessary to practice discernment in our relationship with the emotional and mental components of our being.

We learned to relate to our inner process from a reversed perspective. We were trained to be emotionally dis-honest (that is, to not feel the feelings or to go to the other extreme by allowing the feelings to totally run our lives) and to give power to, to buy into, the reversed attitudes (it is shameful to be human, it is bad to make mistakes, God is punishing and judgmental etc.). To find balance within we have to change our relationship with our inner process.

Feeling and releasing the emotional energy without giving power to the false beliefs is a vital component of achieving balance between the emotional and the mental. The more we align ourselves attitudinally, and clear out our inner channel, the easier it is for us to pick out the Truth from amid the dysfunctional attitudes—so that we can set an internal boundary between the emotional and mental.

Feelings are real but they are not necessarily fact or Truth.

We can feel like a victim and still know that the fact is we set ourselves up. We can feel like we made a mistake and still know that every mistake is an opportunity for growth, a perfect part of the learning process. We can feel betrayed or abandoned or shamed, and still know that we have just been given an opportunity to become aware of an area that needs some light shined on it, an issue that needs some healing.

We can have moments where we feel like God/life is punishing us and still know that "This, too, shall pass" and "More will be revealed,"—that later on, down the path a ways, we will be able to look back and see that what we perceived in the moment to be tragedy and injustice is really just another opportunity for growth, another gift of fertilizer to help us grow.

I needed to learn how to set boundaries within, both emotionally and mentally by integrating Spiritual Truth into my process. Because "I feel like a failure" does not mean that is the Truth. The Spiritual Truth is that "failure" is an opportunity for growth. I can set a boundary with my emotions by not buying into the illusion that what I am feeling is who I am. I can set a boundary intellectually by telling that part of my mind that is judging and shaming me to shut up, because that is my disease lying to me. I can feel and release the emotional pain energy at the same time I am telling myself the Truth by not buying into the shame and judgment.

If I am feeling like a "failure" and giving power to the

79

80   "critical parent" voice within that is telling me that I am a failure—then I can get stuck in a very painful place where I am shaming myself for being me. In this dynamic I am being the victim of myself and also being my own perpetrator—and the next step is to rescue myself by using one of the old tools to go unconscious (food, alcohol, sex, etc.). Thus the disease has me running around in a squirrel cage of suffering and shame, a dance of pain, blame, and self-abuse.

By learning to set a boundary with and between our emotional truth, what we feel, and our mental perspective, what we believe—in alignment with the Spiritual Truth we have integrated into the process—we can honor and release the feelings without buying into the false beliefs.

The more we can learn intellectual discernment within, so that we are not giving power to false beliefs, the clearer we can become in seeing and accepting our own personal path. The more honest and balanced we become in our emotional process, the clearer we can become in following our own personal Truth.

No Blame

One of the false beliefs that it is important to let go of, is the belief that we need another person in our lives to make us whole. As long as we believe that someone else has the power to make us happy then we are setting ourselves up to be victims.

A white knight is not going to come charging up to rescue us from the dragon. A princess is not going to kiss us and turn us from a frog into a prince. The Prince and the Princess and the Dragon are all within us. It is not about someone outside of us rescuing us. It is also not about some dragon outside of us blocking our path. As long as we are looking outside to become whole we are setting ourselves up to be victims. As long as we are looking outside for the villain we are buying into the belief that we are the victim.

As little kids we were victims and we need to heal those wounds. But as adults we are volunteers—victims only of our disease. The people in our lives are actors and actresses whom we cast in the roles that would recreate the childhood dynamics of abuse and abandonment, betrayal and deprivation.

We are/have been just as much perpetrators in our adult relationships as victims. Every victim is a perpetrator—because when we are buying into being the victim, when we are giving power to our disease, we are perpetrating on the people around us and on ourselves.

We need to heal the wounds without blaming others. And we need to own the responsibility without blaming ourselves. As was stated earlier—there is no blame here, there are no bad guys. The only villain here is the disease and it is within us.

I want to make it clear that when I say "without blaming others," I do not mean to deny our anger. We need to own and release the anger and rage at our parents, our teachers or ministers or other authority figures, including the concept of God that was forced on us while we were growing up. We do not necessarily need to vent that anger directly to them but we need to release the energy. We need to let that child inside of us scream, "I hate you, I hate you," while we beat on pillows or some such thing, because that is how a child expresses anger.

That does not mean that we have to buy into the attitude that they are to blame for everything. We are talking about balance between the emotional and mental here again. Blame has to do with attitudes, with buying into the false beliefs—it does not really have anything to do with the process of releasing the emotional energy.

We also need to own and release the anger against those whom we *feel* victimized us as adults—and we need to

81

82 take responsibility for our side of the street, own our part in whatever dysfunctional dance we did with them.

We need to own, honor, and release the feelings, and take responsibility for them—without blaming ourselves.

On the level of our perspective of the process it is very important to stop buying into the false beliefs that as adults we are victims and someone else is to blame—or that we are to blame because there is something wrong with us.

[One of the things which makes it difficult to discuss this phenomenon of Codependence is that there are multiple levels—multiple perspectives—which are involved in this life experience. Viewing life from a perspective, on the level, of individuals who have experienced racial, cultural, religious, or sexual discrimination or abuse, there are instances in which there has been Truth in the belief of victimization. On the level of the historical human experience, all human beings have been victims of the conditions which caused Codependence. Almost any statement can be shown to be false on some levels and True on other levels, so it is important to realize that the use of discernment is vital to start perceiving the boundaries between different levels.

In the next section, Part Five, when I discuss the Cosmic Perspective and the Cosmic Perfection of this life experience, I will be discussing the paradox, and confusion to human beings, that has been the result of these multiple levels of reality—but I have devoted Part Two and Part Four to discussing the Spiritual growth process and our perspective on that process *because the Cosmic Perfection does not mean crap unless we can start integrating it into our day-to-day life experience.*

In order to start changing life into an easier, more enjoyable experience by attaining some integration and balance in our relationships it is necessary to focus on, and clear up, our relationship with this Spiritual Evolutionary process that we are involved in. On the level of that Spiritual growth process it is vital to let go of the belief in victimization and blaming.]

As I said, the goal of healing is not to become perfect, it is not to "get healed." Healing is a process, not a destination—we are not going to arrive at a place in this lifetime where we are completely healed.

The goal here is to make life an easier and more enjoyable experience while we are healing. The goal is to LIVE. To be able to feel happy, Joyous, and free in the moment, the majority of the time.

To get to a place where we are free to be happy in the moment most of the time, we need to change our perspectives enough to start recognizing Truth when we see or hear it. And the Truth is that we are Spiritual Beings having a human experience that is unfolding perfectly and always has been, there are no accidents, coincidences, or mistakes—so there is no blame to be assessed.

The goal here is to be and enjoy! We can't do that if we are judging and shaming ourselves. We can't do that if we are blaming ourselves or others.

Powerlessness

We must start recognizing our powerlessness over this disease of Codependence.

As long as we did not know we had a choice we did not have one.

If we never knew how to say "no," then we never really said "yes."

We were powerless to do anything any different than we did it. We were doing the best we knew how with the tools that we had. None of us had the power to write a different script for our lives.

We need to grieve for the past. For the ways in which we abandoned and abused ourselves. For the ways we deprived

83

84   ourselves. We need to own that sadness. But we also need to stop blaming ourselves for it. It was not our fault!

We did not have the power to do it any differently.

As long as we are holding onto the guilt and feeling ashamed, it means that on some level we think we had the power. We think that if we would have just done it a little differently, if we had just done it "right," if we could have just said the "right" thing, then we could have controlled it and had it come out the way we wanted.

The part of you that is telling you that is your disease.

The part of you that tells you that you are not lovable, that you are not worthy, that you are not deserving, is the disease. It is trying to maintain control because that is all that it knows how to do.

We are not "better than." We are also not "less than." The messages that we are "better than" come from the same place that the messages of "less than" come from: the disease.

We are all children of God who deserve to be happy.

And if you are right now judging yourself for not being happy enough or healed enough—that is your disease talking. Tell it to fuck off!!

It is not who you are—*it is only a part of you.* We can stop giving power to that part of us. We can stop being the victims of ourselves.

Recovery is a process of learning to forgive ourselves, of making amends to ourselves. It was not our fault.

Healing is, however, our responsibility. Today you know that there are choices—you know that there are resources and groups and tools—or you would not be reading this book.

The part of you that has been making up excuses for not getting more aligned with healing is your disease. Don't judge yourself for it—observe it. Say to yourself, "Oh, isn't that interesting, I don't think I want to do that anymore." Or you can say, "Hey, this denial is still working for me, I think I'll stick with it for awhile." Whatever works to make you happy. (You might want to remember, however, that if you don't follow the carrots—the Universe will use the stick.)

As long as we are judging and shaming ourselves we are giving power to the disease. We are feeding the monster that is devouring us.

We need to take responsibility without taking the blame. We need to own and honor the feelings without being a victim of them.

We need to rescue and nurture and Love our inner children—and STOP them from controlling our lives. STOP them from driving the bus! Children are not supposed to drive, they are not supposed to be in control.

And they are not supposed to be abused and abandoned. We have been doing it backwards. We abandoned and abused our inner children. Locked them in a dark place within us. And at the same time let the children drive the bus—let the children's wounds dictate our lives.

We were powerless out of ego-self to do anything any different than we did it. We are powerless out of ego-self to heal this disease. Through Spiritual Self, through our Spiritual Connection, we have access to all the power in the Universe.

We need to have the willingness: willingness to get to a new level of self-honesty; willingness to start listening to the Loving inner voice instead of the shaming ones; willingness to face the terror of healing the emotional wounds.

Codependence causes us to have a distorted and repressed emotional process, and the only way out is through the feelings. Codependence gives us a scrambled mind, a reversed dysfunctional way of looking at ourselves and the world, and we have to be able to use the wonderful tool that is our mind while changing our attitudes and reprogramming our thinking.

85

It seems awfully complicated, doesn't it?

That is because it is!

On another level it is also very simple. It is a Spiritual Disease. It can only be healed through a Spiritual Cure. It cannot be healed by only looking at the symptoms. That is backwards.

The cure is available through surrendering control to a Higher Power. We cannot do this healing by ourselves. We need a Loving Higher Power in our lives. We need other Recovering people in our lives.

We are powerless out of human ego-self to get out of this quagmire. That is the bad news. It is also the good news.

Once you let go enough times, once you becoming willing to go to any length, to do whatever it takes, once you become willing to make healing the number one priority in your life, then you will be guided all the way. You will get the tools you need when you need them. You will get the help you need when you need it. You will have Loving, supportive people come into your life when you need them. You will start making rapid, discernible progress in your healing transformation.

On the other side of powerlessness is all the power in the Universe. On the other side of powerlessness is freedom, happiness, and peace within. On the other side of powerlessness is Joy and Love!

The answer is to stop fighting it, to surrender to the Spiritual Forces at work. Surrender to the possibility that maybe, just maybe, you do deserve to be happy and Loved.

The Death of the Ego

We need to let go of the illusion that we can control this life business. We cannot. We never could! It was an illusion. And we need to let go of the false beliefs that tell us that we are bad and shameful. We cannot become whole as long as we believe that any part of us is bad or shameful.

That includes the ego—that bloated out-of-balance dragon within. Thank God for our egos, they are what allowed us to survive. Thank God for Codependence, without it we would not be alive. But now is the time to get things into balance—the time to bring ego-self into alignment and balance with Spiritual Self.

That is the transformation which is known as "the death of the ego." To quote the *St. Francis Prayer*, "It is through dying that we awaken to eternal life." It is not referring just to physical death, it is referring to the death of the ego which allows us to awaken to the Truth of eternal life.

The death of the ego is not an event—it is a process. It is not an act of violence—it is an act of Love. A process of learning to Love.

We are bringing ego-self into alignment with Spiritual Truth. We are reconnecting with our Spiritual nature and Spiritual purpose so that we can find some fulfillment and happiness in life.

Our Purpose

We are Spiritual Beings and we are here in these bodies, at this time, to do this healing.

So the bad news is that the world is a real mess because we have been doing it all backwards. The good news is that it was all part of the Divine Script and that the healing has begun.

The good news individually is that the dance is changing, the healing and Joy are available to us now. The bad news individually (from an emotional perspective) is that in order to do this healing, it is necessary to do our grief processing, to feel our feelings. It is necessary to go through the black hole.

That is the reason we came into body in this lifetime—to go through that black hole, to do this healing!

The time has come for you to remember that. This is your wake-up call. It is not the first and it probably will not be the last. But it is not an accident or a coincidence that you are reading this today.

It is time to stop the nonsense of believing that our purpose and meaning comes from the money, or the job, or the relationship. We are here to be a part of the Transformational Healing Process that has begun on this planet—we are here to heal our relationship with ourselves, with our wounded souls.

The time has come to stop doing it backwards. It is time to stop shaming and abusing an innocent child, to stop judging and blaming an innocent Adult Child. The time has come to start Loving yourself.

We are Spiritual Beings having a human experience.

We are butterflies having a caterpillar experience.

We are swans having an ugly duckling experience.

We are not going to slay the dragon. We are going to Love it and reduce it in size.

Love is the secret weapon in this war! Learning to Love ourselves, and remembering that the God-Force Loves us, is what will bring peace within.

In closing this section I am going to share a story that I heard at a Twelve Step meeting. It is a story about a parent and a child.

This was one of those times when the parent was busy with something that needed to be done and the child was bored and wanted some attention. The parent needed to concentrate and was desperate to find something to distract the child for a little while so that the parent could get done with what needed to be done and could then give the child some attention. In glancing around, the parent noticed a large fold out map of the world from a magazine. The parent took the map of the world and cut it up into pieces and gave it to the child along with some scotch tape and said, "Here honey, why don't you see how quickly you can put this map of the world together."

The child liked this idea and quickly went to work. The parent was sure that this little ploy had bought some valuable time to get finished with the project at hand. But in only a very few minutes the child called out that the map was all put together. The parent could not believe it and went over to where the child was sitting on the floor and was astounded to see the map all put together.

"How did you do that so fast?!" The parent asked.

The child, looking a little sheepish, said, "Well, I kinda cheated a little. On the other side of the map of the world was the picture of a person. *I just put the person together and the world came together all by itself.*"

That's what this Recovery process is all about. If we just focus on putting ourselves together the world will take care of itself.

Ye shall know the Truth,
and the Truth shall make you free.

JOHN 8:32

The wolf also shall dwell with
the lamb, and the leopard shall lie down
with the kid:...and a little
child shall lead them.

ISAIAH 11:6

God (Goddess, Great Spirit,
Allah, etc.) grant me the serenity
to accept the things I cannot change,
the courage to change the things I can,
and the wisdom to know the difference.

SERENITY PRAYER

CHAPTER FIVE
THE COSMIC PERSPECTIVE

The way we change the dance of Codependence to the dance of Recovery, the way we tame the dragon inside, is through integration and balance. One of the ways we do that is by stopping the dysfunctional behavior of looking for the Prince or Princess who is going to fix us and make us whole.

The Prince and the Princess exist within. That Prince, the Masculine Energy of Manifestation and Action, and that Princess, the Feminine Energy of Creativity and Nurturing, exist within us in perfect balance and harmony. They always have—and they always will.

As has been stated, we are not broken—we do not need fixing. It is our relationship with ourselves which needs to be healed; it was our sense of self that was shattered and fractured and broken into pieces—not our True Self. Recovery is a process of awakening to, of becoming conscious of, the perfect balance and harmony that has always been and always will be—of learning to accept a state of Grace—and integrating that Truth into our lives.

The feeling of being broken is not fact. It is an illusion. The dysfunction is the result of illusion. The disease of Codependence is caused by illusion.

The original wound, the genesis of all the pain in the human experience, the original cause from which Codependence emerged, is the illusion that we are separate from God, from our Creator.

We are not. We never have been. But due to planetary

91

92 conditions it felt like we were. It felt like being human was a punishment.

The incredible pain of feeling separate from the Creative Source is the greatest pain there is.

The original wound was feeling abandoned by God. Feeling betrayed by the Creator. It was the feeling that the Source from which we sprang, The Universal Creative Intelligence, had abandoned us, which caused humans to assume that we had done something shameful enough to be punished.

This human business we are experiencing is an illusion. A gigantic, multi-dimensional hologram projected forth vibrationally in the imagination of the God-Force.

It is a *dream of creation*. We are in the process of awakening from that Creation Dream.

Physics

One of the fascinating things about the Age of Healing and Joy that has dawned in human consciousness is that the tools and knowledge that we need to raise our consciousness, to awaken to consciousness, have been unfolding in all areas of human endeavor over time, and at an accelerated rate in the last fifty to one hundred years.

One of the most fascinating things to me, and a key in my personal healing process, is in the area of physics.

Physicists have now proven through Einstein's Theory of Relativity and the study of quantum physics that everything we see is an illusion.

Einstein, in looking at a macroscopic perspective of the Universe, said in his Theory of Relativity that there are more than three dimensions. Human beings can only visualize in three dimensions. We can only see three dimensions so we have assumed that that is all there is.

Einstein also stated that time and space are not the

absolute variables that science has traditionally believed them to be—that they are, in fact, a relative experience.

Quantum physics, the study of the microscopic, the subatomic world, has gone even further. Quantum physics has now proven that everything we see is an illusion, that the physical world is an illusion.

Everything is made up of interacting energy. Energy interacts on a subatomic level to form energy fields which physicists call subatomic particles. These subatomic energy fields interact to form atomic energy fields, atoms, which interact to form molecules. Everything in the physical world is made up of interacting atomic and molecular energy fields.

There is no such thing as separation in the physical world.

Energy is interacting to form a gigantic, dynamic pattern of rhythmically repeating energy interactions. In other words, a dance of energy. We are all part of a gigantic dance of energy.

This Universe is one gigantic pattern of dancing energy patterns.

Separation is an illusion. There is energy traveling at thousands of miles per second in your body right at this moment. There is energy interacting between, passing between, you and the chair you are sitting on, you and the air around you, you and any other beings in the room.

We are not separate.

Physicists have scientifically proven that separation in the physical world is an illusion. They have scientifically proven that all the basic assumptions upon which traditional science is based, are false.

We are all part of one gigantic, dynamic dance of energy.

ONENESS is the Truth, the scientifically proven Truth, on this physical plane. It is also the Truth on multiple levels through multi-dimensional interrelationships.

All the pieces of the puzzle fit together perfectly

93

according to logical, rational, precise, mathematically and musically attuned laws of energy interaction. When we look at the life experience in a large enough perspective we can remember that.

The mystical Truth that we are all ONE in God has been known through the ages. What we have never had before is the ability to integrate that mystical Truth into human physical, perceptual reality.

We now have the tools and the knowledge that we need to do that. We now have the guidance we need to integrate Spiritual Truth into physical experiential reality. To find a place of balance in the physical world in alignment with Spiritual Truth.

Levels

One of the reasons that our perception of, and relationship with, this life business has been so out-of-balance is that we have lacked the ability to discern between different levels. The twisted, distorted perspective of life that humans have evolved is, in part at least, the result of trying to apply the Truths of one level to the reality of another.

Several examples of this distortion phenomena can be drawn from the archetypal images which were used at the beginning of this section: the Prince and the Princess. Symbolically the image of the Prince and the Princess can be interpreted on many levels.

One level is, of course, as symbols of the Masculine and Feminine Energy of Creation. The marriage of the Princess and the Prince can on this level be seen to represent the Feminine and Masculine Principles of the Universe and their union of perfect balance and harmony—the eternal balance of yin and yang. So on this level, "happily ever after" is the Truth.

This perfect union symbolizes on an individual level the attaining of integration and balance between the masculine and feminine energies within. It is the process of striving for integration and balance of masculine and feminine within (integration of Spiritual Truth into our relationship with our mental, emotional, and physical levels, balance between mental and emotional, between rational and intuitive, between feeling and thinking) that allows us to find some balance and harmony in our relationships with ourselves and with life. This striving for integration and balance (which working a Twelve Step program brings to an individual's life—even if one is not conscious that that is what is happening) allows us to reach a place where we can be happy in the moment the majority of the time—happy, Joyous, and free. So there is some Truth on this level in "happily ever after."

The coming into balance of the Feminine and Masculine Principles in their manifestation into interrelationships on the planet (as was stated, they have always been perfectly in balance but that perfect balance still needs to be integrated into human interactions) which will arise out of the healing being done on a personal level, is what will allow the world to evolve into a peace-full environment. Again Truth in "happily ever after."

Another level has to do with the Spiritual Truth that at the culmination of the Spiritual Evolutionary process each of us will be united with our Twin Soul, and will then be finished with Karma and painful lessons, so that we can live happily ever after—that is, consciously realize Eternal existence in a state of Joy and Bliss.

So we have four levels, perspectives, on which "happily ever after" is a concept that contains at least some Truth. However, applying that Truth to the physical plane in the form of believing that you will achieve "happily ever after" when you get married or find your mate is obviously a false and dysfunctional belief that has resulted from human inability to discern between levels.

95

Human beings have also tried to apply realities of the physical level to the Spiritual level with the disastrous result that humans have come up with an image of the God-Force that fights wars. This image of the God-Force, with the characteristics of a war-like male, is completely out of balance because it is not the image of a balanced male warrior—*it is the image of a male with no feminine side.*

As has been stated there is some Truth in everything. There is some Truth in the image of the Creative Force being masculine. Masculine energy governs manifestation, and the Creation was an act of manifestation, so it was a Masculine act. What the image of a masculine god ignores, however, is the Truth that, though the creative action is Masculine, the creative urge is Feminine. Therefore, even though the act of Creation may have been a Masculine manifestation, a father thing if you will, prior to the creative act existed the urge, which means that the Feminine principle, mother or goddess energy if you will, preceded the masculine.

This inability to discern between different levels of reality is part (along with the planetary conditions which will be addressed shortly) of the reason that many religious teachings are twisted, distorted, grotesquely warped misinterpretations of what were originally symbolic, metaphoric, allegorical attempts to explain the unexplainable.

Western Civilization (in reaction to earlier ages when it was out of balance to the other extreme of allowing superstition to rule) does not acknowledge that multiple levels of reality exist and as a result, has been way out of balance towards the left brain way of thinking—rational, logical, concrete, what you see is all there is. Since what is seen is a three dimensional illusion, anything that does not fit neatly into that three dimensional world has been labeled as not being real. Logically then, according to Western thought, the supernatural does not exist—it is only imagination and superstition—therefore anyone who believes in the supernatural is crazy.

Because emotional energy could not be seen or measured or weighed, and was not sanctioned by the AMA, emotions were discounted and devalued.

Western Civilization has discounted anything that does not fit into the three dimensional framework, into a single perspective that twists, distorts, and enmeshes the levels of reality, and has shamed, ridiculed, and persecuted the individuals and groups who challenged this rigidly rational perspective.

At the same time Western Civilization has been based on insane, irrational concepts like "love is shameful and manipulative" and "god is a male who fights wars."

It is a pretty backwards way of doing things.

Paradox

It is vitally important to start recognizing that different levels of reality exist, and to clear out our emotional process so that we can discern Truth and throw out the garbage.

There are supernatural phenomena. There are other levels of reality beyond the natural three dimensional view. This Illusion contains multiple levels of illusions which are all interrelated and interdependent; which are all, in some way—direct, indirect, or symbolic—reflections of each other.

Everything is interdependent and interrelated; everything outside of us is a reflection of what is within.

When we look at reality from a different perspective, on a higher level, in a larger context, then we can start seeing how what we perceive as tragedy on one level, can fit into the plan perfectly on a higher level. How it is a perfect part of the larger picture, of a longer journey. Then we can begin to understand how the pieces of the puzzle fit together.

The Twelve Step Recovery process is so successful because it provides a formula for integrating different levels. It is by recognizing that we are powerless to control our life experiences out of ego-self that we can access the power out of True Self, Spiritual Self. By surrendering the illusion of ego control we can reconnect with our Higher Selves. Selfishness out of ego-self is destroying the planet. Selfishness out of Spiritual Self is what will save the planet.

It is because there is more than one level of reality that life is paradoxical in nature. What is True and positive on one level—selfishness out of Spiritual Self, can be negative on another level—selfishness out of ego-self. What a caterpillar calls the end of the world, God calls a butterfly.

Humans have always had expressions that describe the paradoxical nature of the life experience. Every ending is a beginning. Every cloud does have a silver lining. For every door that closes, another door does open. It is always darkest before the dawn. Every obstacle is a gift, every problem is an opportunity for growth.

These are all expressions that refer to the paradoxical nature of life—the seeming contradictions that are a result of the multiple levels of reality. When we start to understand and recognize that there are multiple levels of reality, then we can begin to unravel the paradox and see how all of the pieces fit together perfectly.

One of the gifts that came to me early in my healing process was a little expression that helped me start changing my perspective. That expression was, "I don't have any problems—I have opportunities for growth." The more I stopped focusing on problems and obstacles, and started looking for the gifts, the lessons attached to them, the easier life became.

I became a part of the solution instead of getting stuck being the victim of the problem. I started seeing the half of the glass that was full instead of always focusing on the half that was empty.

Every problem is an opportunity for growth.

My subconscious Codependent attitudes and perspectives caused me to take life personally—to react emotionally as if life events were being directed at me personally as a punishment for being unworthy, for being a shameful creature.

Life is a series of lessons. The more I became aligned with knowing that I was being given gifts to grow from—the less I believed that the purpose of life was to punish me—the easier life became.

Everything happens for a reason; *there is always a silver lining.*

The Silver Lining

I am now going to share with you an example of how everything without is a reflection to us of what needs to be healed within; an example of how all of the pieces of the puzzle do fit together; an example of how even the darkest cloud can have a silver lining—if we look for it.

It is no accident, from a cosmic perspective, that in the last fifteen or sixteen years, as we have been coming to a new understanding of our Spiritual dis-ease, we have received a problem/gift that is a reflection of that disease on the physical level.

I am referring to AIDS—Acquired Immune Deficiency Syndrome.

From a human standpoint AIDS is a great tragedy, a profound injustice. However, if we look at it from the larger perspective, we can see how it fits into the puzzle. We can see the silver lining. The tragedy of AIDS has brought gifts with it.

On an individual level it has provided opportunities for healing, for Spiritual Awakening, and for Karmic settlement for those Souls who, for reasons in alignment with Divine purpose, chose to make AIDS a part of their path in this lifetime.

In a larger context, in terms of society as a whole, it has forced us to take a close look at death, at the dying process. It has brought death out of the darkness in a way, and forced

99

us to stop ignoring its eventuality. It has brought the dying process out of the dark into the Light in a way that no other disease has or could have.

It has also caused us to learn more about the grieving process. It has helped us to rediscover this invaluable tool.

And, maybe most importantly, it has forced us on an individual level to stop substituting physical intimacy for emotional intimacy. Trying to get our emotional needs met through sex does not work. It is dysfunctional. Human sexuality is a blessed gift when it is in balance with the emotional, mental and Spiritual. This is an emotionally dishonest society which knows very little about True, healthy emotional intimacy. The tragedy of AIDS brought with it the gift of forcing us to start learning about emotional intimacy.

Over and beyond these gifts that the injustice of AIDS brought with it, it is also a blatantly direct reflection of what these wounds we are healing are all about.

AIDS is a disease caused by the physical body's immune system, its defense system, breaking down, becoming dysfunctional, to the extent that the body's very defense system aids and abets in the destruction of the physical body vehicle.

Codependence is a disease which involves the being's emotional defense system being dysfunctional to the extent that it breaks our hearts and destroys our ability to Love and be Loved, wounds our souls by denying us access to our Spiritual Self, and scrambles our minds so thoroughly that it causes our minds to become our own worst enemies.

The dysfunction that is AIDS mutilates the body and causes death.

The dysfunction that is Codependence mutilates the soul/spirit and causes us to walk around dead inside—and eventually also causes physical death.

AIDS is a fatal disease of the body—Codependence is a fatal disease of the spirit and the body.

Everything is interrelated and interdependent. Everything without is a reflection of within. All of the pieces of the puzzle fit together.

Summer Camp

As was stated earlier, Codependence is a functional defense system only in terms of physical survival of the species—it was necessary as long as physical survival was the first priority. The conditions have now changed on the planet. Physical survival is no longer the first priority. Physical existence, like death, is an illusion.

We had to go unconscious in order to survive the emotional pain. Thank God for the survival tool that is denial—without it we would not still be here in this lifetime. As has been stated, thank God for the emotional/behavioral defense system that is Codependence—without it we could not have survived.

But now, in the Age of Healing and Joy that has dawned in human consciousness, our first priority is Spiritual Awakening.

This healing process is why we are here!

The awakening to consciousness of our Spiritual nature and Spiritual purpose is why we are here at this time.

This is the age of awakening, of raising our consciousness, of becoming aligned with Divine Truth. This age is the time of atoning, of tuning into the higher vibrational emotional energy of Love, Light, Truth, and Joy. This higher vibrational energy is the homing beacon that guides us back home.

There is a reason that we never felt at home here. It is because we have felt disconnected, and then when we made all those attempts to reconnect, we were dialing the wrong number. We were looking outside for the answers.

This is not home. This is also not a prison. *This is boarding school and we are getting ready for graduation.* And it is all a perfect part of the Divine Script.

We are here to experience this human evolutionary process. The more we awaken to the Truth of who we are (Spiritual beings) and why we are here (to experience being human), and stop giving power to the false gods of money, property and prestige; people, places and things; *the more we can celebrate being here!*

Buddha had it half right: We need to let go of our attachment to the illusions of this Illusion. But as we stop giving power to the illusions, we can begin to celebrate being here, we can begin to enjoy our human experience.

This is a playground, this is a wonderful summer camp. It is full of beautiful colors and wondrous sights, animals and birds and plants, mountains and oceans and meadows, whales and butterflies. It is full of tastes and smells and sounds and sensations.

The gift of touch is an incredibly wonderful gift. One of the reasons we are here is to touch each other physically as well as Spiritually, emotionally, and mentally. Touch is not bad or shameful. Our creator did not give us sensual and sexual sensations that feel so wonderful just to set us up to fail some perverted, sadistic life test. Any concept of god that includes the belief that the flesh and the Spirit cannot be integrated, that we will be punished for honoring our powerful human desires and needs, is—in my belief—a sadly twisted, distorted, and false concept that is reversed to the Truth of a Loving God-Force.

We need to strive for balance and integration in our relationships. We need to touch in healthy, appropriate, emotionally honest ways—so that we can honor our human bodies and the gift that is physical touch.

Making Love is a celebration and a way of honoring the Masculine and Feminine Energy of the Universe (and the masculine and feminine energy within no matter what genders are involved), a way of honoring its perfect interaction and harmony. It is a blessed way of honoring the Creative Source.

One of the most blessed and beautiful gifts of being in body is the ability to feel on a sensual level. Because we have been doing human backwards, we have been deprived of the pleasure of enjoying our bodies in a guilt-free, shame-free, manner. By striving for integration and balance we can start to enjoy our human experience—on a sensual level as well as on the emotional, mental, and Spiritual levels.

As we learn the dance of Recovery, as we tune into the energy of Truth, we can reverse our emotional experience of being human so that most of the time it can feel more like a wonderful summer camp than a dreadful prison.

Molecular Biology

We have been doing this human business backwards. *The reason we have been doing it backwards is that the energy field of Collective Human Emotional Consciousness on planet Earth was reversed in its relationship to Truth for tens of thousands of years. It is not reversed anymore!*

As I stated earlier, the knowledge that we need to understand the larger perspective has been unfolding in all areas of human endeavor. That includes the field of molecular biology. Biologists have discovered a phenomenon that is mind-boggling. They call it a morphogenetic field, or M-field. This is an energy field of consciousness. They have discovered energy fields of consciousness exist not only for animals but also for objects we think of as inanimate, such as crystals.

A biologist named Lyall Watson coined a term having to do with this phenomenon. That term is the "hundredth monkey effect." This is the story of how the term came about, as related in *Beyond The Quantum* by Michael Talbot.

Watson relates an unusual incident that allegedly occurred in the 1950s in a population of Japanese mon-

103

keys known as *Macaca fuscata* on the island of Koshima just off the east coast of Kyushu. It seems that while studying the local population of these monkeys, researchers started feeding them sweet potatoes and would dump truckloads of them on the beach for the monkeys to retrieve. The problem was that although the monkeys had developed elaborate feeding habits for all of their indigenous foods, they had never seen sweet potatoes before. Their dilemma was not that they did not like the new treat, but that the sweet potatoes were covered with sand and grit—an unpleasant problem that the monkeys had never before confronted.

As Watson tells the story, the monkeys struggled with the problem for awhile, like picnickers assailed by ants, and then an eighteen-month-old female, a sort of monkey genius the researchers knew as Imo, solved the dilemma. Imo discovered that if the gritty sweet potatoes were dunked in the ocean, not only did it remove the sand, but it added an interesting new flavor. Imo next taught the trick to her mother, then her playmates, and slowly the new habit gained a small following in the Koshima colony.

Then something remarkable transpired. As Watson relates, the details of what happened next have not yet been published because the primate researchers involved knew that what they would be disclosing was too heretical for general scientific consumption. It seems that one morning the number of monkeys that had learned Imo's washing technique reached a sort of critical mass, and then, suddenly, by that evening, every monkey in the colony was washing potatoes in the surf. Not only that, but researchers reported that troops of monkeys on other islands and even a troop on the mainland at Takasakiyama also suddenly and spontaneously began practicing Imo's washing technique. Although the researchers on

Koshima had not observed at precisely what number of monkeys this critical mass was reached, for the sake of speaking about it Watson refers to the monkey individual that put the entire population over the threshold as the proverbial "hundredth monkey."

Biologists found that principles which were known to apply in physics also applied in biology in certain ways. An electromagnetic energy field can only accept a certain amount of energy of a reversed polarity—that is, if the energy is positive it can only accept so much negative and vice-versa—until it reaches a decisive point that is called critical mass. When a negative energy field reaches critical mass it reverses and the whole field goes positive.

What these biologists discovered is that an energy field of consciousness existed for these monkeys, and that when enough of the monkeys, the "hundredth monkey," had adopted a new survival technique, *their energy field of consciousness reached a point of critical mass and altered to make that new technique, that new survival tool, available to all of the monkeys of that species.*

Energy Fields

Energy fields of consciousness exist. Energy fields of intellectual and emotional consciousness for humans exist in relationship to every type of relationship, of interaction, that humans experience.

Each human being is an energy field, made up of interacting atomic and molecular energy fields. When people come together they form a group energy field. Groups have incredible power because they form a more powerful energy field than an individual does. It is sometimes easier to access the higher vibrational transcendent emotions in a group than as an individual.

That is why it feels good, why it feels like the energy is powerful and positive in most Twelve Step meetings, and in some churches and Spiritual gatherings, because it is. It is a higher vibrational energy field.

Whenever two or more are gathered in the name of Love and Truth, in the name of healing, there is incredible power.

Any single soul's evolution, its awakening, affects all souls because we are all connected. We can, like Imo the genius monkey, create a space, create a new level—a new aspect—of consciousness that other humans then have access to. It is not any accident that most great inventions, most great breakthroughs, were formulated in more than one location in the same time period. Once one breaks through and creates the space, others may follow.

A single soul's healing advances the healing of all souls—imagine the power of two or more.

The effects of group healing and awakening ripple out through human consciousness to affect all Souls. It ripples out in geometric proportion.

Polarization

The energy field of Collective Human Emotional Consciousness on this planet was reversed in relationship to the Truth of the God-Force because of the polarization of the energy field of Collective Human Intellectual Consciousness.

The Lower Mind.

Polarization, *the tree of knowledge of good and evil,* caused humans to see life, both externally and internally, as a battle of warring polar opposites: black and white thinking.

The polarization of the Lower Mind caused the connection to the Higher Mind to be weakened. It caused static and distortion to disrupt the channel between human self and Spiritual Self.

This polarization created the illusion of disconnection,

of separation. It caused the Spiritual Beings who were in human body at the time to start focusing on the external reality of the illusion so much that they did not even notice that they were losing their connection to the God-Force. They eventually forgot that they were connected to the God-Force and began to believe that they were individual human beings who existed as entities separate from an external Source. They forgot that the power that they had access to came from the Spirit and not just from themselves. Eventually, (after The Flood) they would even come to believe that they had the power to cause separation—that they were powerful enough to have done something so bad that God would abandon and punish them.

The Truth is that we are powerless to separate from the God-Force because separation is an illusion. Free will is an illusion on the highest level. No being has the power to separate from the ONENESS of God.

It is necessary and healthy to take responsibility for our choices, to accept our consequences, and to try to make healthy decisions on a human level. Integration and balance involve a process of learning to accept healthy responsibility on a human level at the same time that we know we are being guided by a Loving Spiritual Force.

The Force is with us!

It does not mean we can sit back and do nothing. It also does not mean we have to do everything. Either way is out of balance. We have to plant the seeds, and nurture the garden. It is in the growth that the miracle occurs. Whether or not the seed becomes a rose is in the Great Spirit's hands. We are powerless to turn a seed into a rose without the Goddess.

We are powerless out of human ego-self over this life business. We have access to all of the power in the Universe out of our Spiritual Self—out of our Spiritual connection to Higher Consciousness.

107

As a direct result of polarization, the energy field of Collective Human Emotional Consciousness on the planet—which was then in positive alignment with Truth—started to become polluted with negative energy. The human race increasingly manifested behavior that was in opposition, was reversed, to the Truth of Love—until that energy field of emotional consciousness reached critical mass in relationship to Truth, and reversed from a polarity that was in positive alignment with the Truth of the God-Force to a polarity that was negative, that was reversed.

I stated earlier that Codependence was a new name for the tune that we have been dancing to. What it used to be called was *the war between good and evil.*

Evil is the negative polarity. It is that which is reversed to the Truth of the Goddess. It is doing life backwards.

The word evil is live spelled backwards.

There are no accidents, no coincidences.

Evil is an illusion. Maya is a Hindu word that means both illusion and evil. Evil only exists within The Illusion. Evil always was an illusion within The Illusion.

A war between God and the forces of evil is a ridiculous concept. War is evil: It is reversed to the Truth of Love. How could a good God engage in evil, reversed activity, to fight evil which is the illusionary effect of "reversity"?!

Why would an all-powerful Creative Source need to fight anything? It is a ridiculous concept that only had power because the human perspective on life was polarized and reversed.

Back To the Light

Onto this planet of reversed consciousness teachers were sent. They carried the message of ONENESS so that the reversed energy field could start the process of returning to positive.

There were many of these teachers. They taught ONENESS. They taught Truth. But because the planetary energy field of consciousness was reversed, even they did not have clear unobstructed connection with the Higher Mind, with their Spiritual Self. Because of enmeshment on a personal level between ego-self and Spiritual-Self, they mixed distortion and misinformation in with the Truth they preached.

Even their messages became polarized between those who humanized God into one supreme being with physical attributes, and those who tried to explain the wholeness, the yin/yang, of the dynamic life process by symbolically naming different aspects, different manifestations of the interaction. This second approach deteriorated in many cases into pantheons of numerous separate individual gods at odds with each other.

Their messages contained Truth but also became twisted and distorted. It did not matter: The process of returning to positive alignment with the Light had begun.

Buddha carried Truth and served as a messenger for teaching people how to protect themselves until it was time to awaken. [In the context of today's healing, it can be seen that Buddha's fourth great truth (one must control conduct, thinking, and belief) can be interpreted as referring to developing internal and external boundaries, practicing discernment, choosing an enlightened perspective, and having an honest, balanced emotional relationship with self. The need to choose right views, right conduct, right effort, etc., in this context can be seen to refer to integration and balance—not right versus wrong.]

Others taught different degrees and aspects of ONENESS. However, because this was a time of reversity and polarization those who did attempt to own the power of the Light and be messengers of Truth met one of two fates. These teachers either were punished for speaking Truth—by being beheaded, stoned, or crucified, etc., or they themselves became twisted and arrogant and ended up serving the darkness instead of the Light. After starting out with teaching Truth, they ended up serving evil because of the planetary conditions.

Even the messages of the Master Teachers who managed to stay aligned with Truth, and were put to death for it, did not survive. Their messages became twisted and distorted by their followers or people claiming to be their followers—so that religions and groups formed in their names ended up serving the darkness in the name of those Master Teachers and the messages of Truth that they had carried.

Because everything was reversed it makes logical sense that the teachings of one of the most important Master Teachers in the history of humanity would be the teacher whose name has been most abused. Actually most of us know very little of what this very important Master Teacher really taught because his teachings were so completely twisted and distorted shortly after his death.

The man who was primarily responsible for distorting those teachings was not even a follower of this teacher, nor had he ever met him—but he was successful in using this teacher's name to form the *biggest multi-national conglomerate ever to serve evil*. The corporate religion that was formed in the name of this Master Teacher—though it also did much good and even in serving evil was a perfect part of the Divine plan—has been the single most enduring and obstructive organization to serve the darkness in the name of Light and Truth that has ever existed.

Up until this very day this Master Teacher's name is being taken in vain by bigoted, racist, small-minded people—very sick, controlling, Codependents with very terrified, very wounded inner children—who act in ways that are the very reverse from this man's teachings.

The coming of this Master Teacher 2000 years ago was a

milestone in the journey that marked a great acceleration in the process of moving back to alignment with the Light within.

This Master Teacher was known as Jesus the Christ. The man Jesus was a perfect child of the Goddess and God energy—just as we all are perfect children of the God-Force!

This messenger added the most powerful ingredient to the process. He brought us our secret weapon. He taught Love. He carried the message of a Loving God.

[The man Paul, who laid the groundwork for the corporate religion, in his search for understanding of this Master's teachings, decreed that Jesus was not just an enlightened human being. He created the myth that Jesus was uniquely different, that he was in fact the "son of God," who had been sent to Earth to save humans from the sin and shame of being human. His teachings, which Christianity evolved out of, promoted the lie that the flesh and the Spirit were incompatible and that being human was shameful. (Those teachings, of course, arose out of the shame that he felt about his life.) The effect of Paul's philosophy was to negate and reverse the teachings of Jesus about the power of Love and the Truth of a Loving God.]

The reason that we have not been Loving our neighbor as ourselves is because we have been doing it backwards. We were taught to judge and feel ashamed of ourselves. We were taught to hate ourselves for being human.

We are here to learn to Love ourselves so that we can Truly Love our neighbors. We've been doing it backwards: hating our neighbors like we hate ourselves.

It is kind of a cosmic joke, see. We have been taught that we are human and that it is bad and shameful, and that we have to somehow earn the right to be Spiritual. The Truth is that we already are Spiritual and there is nothing bad or shameful about "being human."

We are Spiritual Beings having a human experience.

112   We are here to experience feelings and touch and Love. The goal of the healing process is not to reach someplace where we are above all the human experiences and feelings. We are here to feel these feelings.

When we become willing to feel the pain, then we become capable of feeling the Joy. *The Joy of doing this healing is incredible!* Our job is to heal and enJoy. Our job is to *be*. We are here to be human *beings*, not human *doings*.

Our job is to follow the Joy to the Truth. Our job is to feel in the moment.

As long as we are reacting to old wounds and old tapes we cannot respond to the now. The more we heal, the more responsibility we have—that is, ability to respond. The ability to respond in the moment.

By honoring and releasing the sadness and the pain and the anger we can get to the Joy and the Love and the Peace. By stopping the war within we can create world peace. Not today. Probably not in our lifetimes. It will take generations (unless the "hundredth monkey effect" kicks in) but the process has begun!

The planet's energy field of Collective Human Emotional Consciousness is now positively aligned with Truth. Besides the planet, putting the world together is not our job. Our job is to find wholeness within ourselves. Our job is to heal—*that is why we are here.*

Spiritual Warriors

When we surrender trying to control everything out of ego-self then we can start accessing the incredible Universal Power to which we are connected. We are Spiritual Warriors!

"Relinquishing control is the ultimate challenge for the Spiritual Warrior." That's a quote from a book called *The Book of Runes.*

"Anything less than the doing of that which gives you

the most joy is denial." That's from the book called *Medicine Cards*.

"Imagine the universe beautiful and just and perfect.... Then be sure of one thing: the Is has imagined it quite a bit better than you have." That's from Richard Bach's *Illusions*.

This is a process, a process we are going to be involved in for the rest of this lifetime. We will never do it perfectly from a human perspective. But the more we are willing to choose to view life as a growth process, and to feel and remember the Truth within us, the more we will become conscious of the Truth that we are perfectly where we are supposed to be on our Spiritual Path—*and that we are being guided Home.*

There is Truth all around us. *And the Truth is setting us free.*

Through healing the inner child, we access Truth and Love. *And the little child shall lead them.*

A Transformational Healing Movement

The prologue to Richard Bach's *Illusions* contains a story about a colony of creatures clinging to the bottom of a stream. Here is a paraphrasing of that story.

> One day one of those creatures became bored with the life of clinging and decided to see what would happen if he let go and got swept up into the stream. He wanted to see where the stream would carry him.
>
> All of the other creatures laughed at him and made fun of him. "You can't let go of the rocks, you'll just get battered and bruised!" "It's insane to let go of the rocks!"
>
> This creature, though, wanted more out of life than just clinging to the rocks. He wanted to find out where the stream went. So he let go of the rocks—and sure enough he got battered and bruised and had to grab ahold again.

113

All of the other creatures ridiculed and laughed at him.

But he said, "I am going to try again. I believe that the stream knows where it is going. I want to see where the stream will take me." So he let go again— and he got battered and bruised again. And then he let go again, and again, and again.

Each time he got a little less battered and bruised. Each time he got a little closer to being swept up in the stream.

Then finally one day he had let go enough times that he did get swept up into the stream. He was caught in the flow of the stream and swept forward.

He was flying!

As he flew along with his heart full of Joy and excitement he passed over another colony of clinging creatures that was downstream.

They looked up at him and cried, "Behold! There is a creature like us and he is flying! It must be the Messiah!"

He looked back at them and shouted as he was heading down stream, "No! You don't understand. You can fly, too, all you have to do is *let go. You are as much messiahs as I am.*"

That is what this is all about! The second coming has begun! Not of "The Messiah," but of a whole bunch of messiahs. The messiah—the liberator—is within us! A liberating, Healing Transformational Movement has begun. "The Savior" does not exist outside of us—"The Savior" exists within.

We are the sons and daughters of God. We, the old souls, who are involved in this Healing Movement, are the second coming of the message of Love.

We have entered what certain Native American prophecies call the Dawning of the Fifth World of Peace. Through focusing on our own healing the planet will be healed.

We all have available to us—within—a direct channel to the Highest Vibrational Frequency Range within The Illusion. That highest range involves consciousness of the Glory of ONENESS. It is called Cosmic Consciousness. *It is called Christ Consciousness.*

This is the energy that Jesus was tuned into, and he stated very plainly, "These things that I do, you can do also."—by atoning, by tuning in.

We have access to the Christ Energy within. We have begun the Second Coming of the message of Love.

The dawning of the Age of Healing and Joy is the dawning of the Fifth World of Peace when humans will learn to walk in balance and harmony.

Now that is some pretty wonderful news, wouldn't you say?

What's the Catch?

But hold it! Let's just stop a minute here and look at this. Why would a Loving God put us through all of this suffering? What is the purpose, huh? Why???

Well, needless to say we can't know all of the reasons, but a few that we can know might help our understanding. Part of the reason for being here is to experience being human. We have all lived multiple lifetimes. We have all experienced every facet of being human.

We are now not just healing our wounds from this lifetime, we are doing Karmic settlement on a massive scale, at a very accelerated rate.

Karma is the Loving, wonderful law of energy interaction which governs human interaction. Like the other levels of Universal Law, it is about cause and effect. In this case, "what you sow, you reap."

Karmic Law dictates that every action of cause on the Physical Plane is paid for with a consequence of effect *on the*

115

116   *Physical Plane.* In other words, no one can end up in the hole,
or in some hell in an afterlife. (Hell is here on earth, and we
have all experienced it already.)

We who are doing this healing are about to graduate
from the school of Karmic human experience. Any minute
now...or any lifetime.

What graduation means is that we can be released from
the Karmic merry-go-round, from the Karmic dance that was
necessary because of polarization and "reversity." It does not
mean that we will cease to exist; that would be a pretty hol-
low victory indeed.

What I believe it means is that when peace prevails,
when the thousand years of peace begins, when a balanced,
harmonious, Spiritually-aligned world evolves, then we can
come back and play with all of our friends. With our Kindred
Spirits and our Soul Mates, and in union with our Twin Soul.

Peace Within

Another of the purposes for being here is to fully realize
the incredible gift of eternal existence in ONENESS in a state
of Joy and Bliss. It is not possible to fully realize, to appreci-
ate, to be grateful for, Joy and Bliss, *unless one has had some
experience of some alternative.*

Now I happen to believe that God went overboard with
this experience stuff. I, personally, from my human perspective, get very upset with the God-Force for having such an
active imagination. I mean, really, did all of this have to last
quite so long and be quite so complicated?

I happen to believe—and I have shared my belief and
my feelings with my Higher Power on many occasions—that
my Higher Power works very slowly. I am not at all crazy
about my Higher Power's sense of timing.

And I have informed my Higher Power many times in
very graphic terms that I feel as if I am being given far more

opportunities for growth than I think I need. In fact, there are days when I choose to call my Higher Power "fucking asshole"—which my Higher Power finds really amusing and cute.

But my Truth is—from the depths of my heart, from my highest levels of honesty—my Truth is, that in those moments when I experience the Joy and the Bliss, the incredible feeling of peace within that I have been able to achieve through my healing process, I can tell you that to me it was all worth it.

All of the pain of this lifetime and all of the other lifetimes.

It was all worth it to Know and to Love.

My life used to be defined by the anger and the pain and the fear; it is not anymore. There is still anger and pain and fear in my life (sometimes a lot more than other times). But now there is a place deep within me that is peaceful even when life is the most painful.

I spent most of my life wanting to die because I thought that was the only way I would ever find any peace. I have peace in my heart today, even when I am feeling that God has abandoned and betrayed me, because on a deeper level *I know* that there is a Loving, Divine plan unfolding.

I enjoy being alive today, in the moment, most of the time.

I am not only glad that I was born, I am overwhelmingly grateful to have the opportunity to be alive at this time in history. And to have the honor and privilege of being a part of this Healing Movement.

This is a Truly Joyous time to be in body!

Karmic Debts

Of course, one of the reasons that I have the honor and privilege of carrying this Joyous message in this lifetime is because of my Karmic debts from other lifetimes.

117

Possibly one of the reasons that you are reading this is because I, personally, owe you a Karmic debt. Maybe I gouged out your eyes when I was a Roman legionnaire or a Viking or something, and now I am repaying that debt by helping you to see more clearly in this lifetime.

We will probably never know for sure and we probably do not have any need to know for sure. Past life information is available to us only on a need-to-know basis. In other words, only if it is directly connected to our healing process in this lifetime. Simple curiosity is not a good enough reason to allow us to access accurate past life information. (Of course we have our curiosity for a reason too.)

Everything happens for a reason—actually for reasons on multiple levels. We can never know all of the reasons. We have no need to know all of the reasons.

What we need to do is to remember that it is all perfect somehow, some way. We need to remember that to help us stop judging ourselves and the process.

As in the quote from *Illusions,* it is the depth of our belief in tragedy and injustice that is a measure of our Spiritual growth. "The depth of our belief" has to do with our perspective, with how much we are buying into the reversed attitudes and false beliefs, with how much power we are giving the illusions.

What I have found is that in many instances even though the levels that I can see, that I am conscious of, are mostly dysfunctional—arising out of the false beliefs and fears of the disease of Codependence—on deeper levels there are "right on" reasons for behaviors for which I was judging myself.

As one simple example, I used to really judge myself and beat myself up because I had a very hard time meditating. I could not get quiet enough inside to do meditation in the "right" way and I thought that that meant there was something wrong with me. I thought that my resistance meant that I was somehow defective. But what was revealed to me was that I had died in meditation in a past life, which made my resistance make sense in a whole new way. (I also came to understand that meditation is about listening to "the small quiet voice"—as prayer is about talking to God—and that it does not necessarily need to be done formally or in the "right" way.)

As another, more universal example, when I started to learn about Codependence, I used to really beat myself up because I found that I was still looking for "her," even though I had learned about some of the dysfunctional levels of that longing.

I had learned that as long as I thought that I needed someone else to make me happy and whole I was setting myself up to be a victim. I had learned that I was not a frog who needed a princess to kiss me in order to turn into a prince—that I am a prince already, and just need to learn to accept that state of Grace, that princeness.

I had come to understand that those levels of my longing were dysfunctional and Codependent—and I judged and shamed myself because I could not let go of the longing for "her."

But as my awakening progressed I realized that there were "right on" reasons for that longing, for that "endless aching need" that I felt.

One of those "right on" levels was that the longing was a message concerning my very real need to attain some balance between the masculine and feminine energy within me—which begets dysfunctional behavior when it is projected, focused, outward as I had been taught to do in childhood.

And on a much deeper level I came to understand that I am—and have been, ever since polarization—looking for my twin soul.

119

As I become discerning I could learn to pick the baby out of the bathwater, that is, not judge and shame myself for longing for "her"—and throw out the dirty bath water, that is, not take action based on, or give power to, the dysfunctional belief that I am a frog who cannot be happy until I find my princess.

By learning discernment we can begin to become conscious of the reasons that are dysfunctional and based on Codependent beliefs and fears (the dirty bathwater) so that we can change the way we react to those levels, can stop giving them power, and we can honor that there are "right on" levels by not shaming or judging ourselves (the baby) *even if we are not sure what those reasons are.*

I am talking about FAITH here.

The more we remember that everything is unfolding perfectly, the more we can have faith that there is a very good reason for even what appears to be the greatest tragedy, the most profound injustice.

We need to accept and honor—that is, not shame and judge ourselves for—not only our feelings and our past behaviors, our human needs and desires, *but also our longings, our resistance, and our fears.*

We have those longings for a reason.

We have those fears and that resistance for a reason.

The more we start remembering that "the Force is with us," the easier it becomes to accept and Love ourselves.

Everything Happens for a Reason

As was stated earlier, maybe the reason you have not done your grief work is that it has not been time yet—everything happens perfectly. Even our procrastination, and our denial, and our avoidance is a perfect part of our path.

We are being guided!

The more we remember that, the easier it is to stop buying into the grandiose, ego-self, arrogant, Codependent, power trip of believing that we have the incredible power to screw up the Great Spirit's Plan. We do not. We never did.

One of the reasons on a very deep level, at a soul/higher ego level, that we have resistance to doing our healing and owning our power is because of our past life experiences.

We have all been punished for owning our power in the past! Whether that was by being burned at the stake for being a healer, or drawn and quartered for being a teacher, or hanged for being a messenger, or whatever.

So we have very good reasons for not trusting God or this life business!

We also have very good reasons for not trusting ourselves because we have all abused the power in the past. We have had lifetimes when we were teachers who led our students astray, when we were healers or leaders or messengers who took the left-hand path and served the forces of darkness instead of Light.

We have very good reasons for being terrified of owning our power again!

Those are the reasons on the deepest level why we have resistance to the healing process; that is why some of us have needed the stick to get us to start awakening.

No matter what our personal stick is, whether it is Alcoholism or love addiction or overeating or whatever, it is the vehicle which has forced us to start awakening. It is the blessed gift that has started our awakening to consciousness of our path.

The conditions on the planet have changed! As long as the planet's energy field of Collective Human Emotional Consciousness was reversed, the process of growing towards the Light attracted the dark.

That is not going to happen this time. The planet's energy field of consciousness is now positively aligned with

121

Truth. *Growing towards the Light now attracts more Light.*

In this age, we can own who we Truly are without feeling as if we are going to be punished for it.

Of course we never really were being punished—it just *felt* like it.

What we have been doing here in human body for all of these lifetimes is receiving the opportunity to experience every facet of the human experience. We have all been creators and destroyers. We have all been the oppressor and the oppressed. We have all been the perpetrator and the victim.

No one has ever done anything to us that we have not done to her/him in some way, at some time.

It is time to stop blaming others. It is time to stop blaming ourselves. We chose the paths we are on in order to do the healing and Karmic settlement that was necessary. We need to own and honor and release the feelings at the same time that we need to stop buying into the false beliefs.

Spiritual Beings

We are Spiritual Beings having a human experience. We are also part of the ONENESS that is God and we helped write the Divine Script.

That's the bad news—it is also the good news.

We have now come to the Joyous part of the story. The dance is changing. It is changing into a dance of healing. It is changing into a dance of Joy, and Love, and Celebration. This is truly a Joyous time to be in body!

The first time a messenger came to me carrying the message, the reminder, that I was a Spiritual Being having a human experience, I got really angry. My first reaction was anger. My first thought was, "That means that I've got to be out among *them.*"

I never wanted to be out among you-all. I always wanted to go up on a mountain and meditate my way to

God. What I have learned in this healing process is that I find God through "being out among them," through my human relationships. We are here to learn to relate to each other. We are here to learn to Love ourselves and each other.

One of the ironies of this whole business is something that physicists have learned from quantum physics. They have learned that the physical world is made up of energy fields that are temporary manifestations of energy interactions. All of the energy fields of the physical world are temporary. Some last for fractions of a second, some last for billions of years—but they are all temporary illusions.

This means that the Truest reality in the physical world is in the interaction. It is in our interactions that we can access Truth and Joy and Love. In other words it is in our relationships.

The most real thing here, the place where the highest Truth exists, is in the interactions: in our relationships. Our relationship with ourselves is a reflection of our relationship with our Creator, with the Great Spirit. And our relationship with ourselves is reflected out into our relationship with everyone and everything in our environment.

Spirituality is about relationships. God exists in the quality of our relationships.

When I look at a beautiful sunset—I am a temporary illusion and the sunset is also a temporary illusion—the most real, God-like quality is the energy of Beauty and Joy that I allow myself to access by being open and willing to experience the sunset. If I am caught up in one of my ego's "trauma dramas," then I will not be conscious of the sunset or open to experiencing the Joy and Beauty of the moment.

A very important part of this healing process is taking time to smell the flowers. Our job is to be here in the now and to do this healing.

I spent most of my life trying to become—perfect, loved,

accepted, respected, etc., etc. It did not work because I was looking outside for something that can only be found within.

Now I know that I am not in control of this process and that what I am becoming is in the hands of a Loving (although somewhat slow-working) Great Spirit. I do not have to worry anymore about becoming—all I have to do is be. I just have to suit up and show up for life today and do what is in front of me. And everything will work out better than I could ever have planned it.

There are no accidents, no coincidences—everything is unfolding perfectly.

It is no accident that two days before I first gave this talk in June of 1991, when I didn't know exactly what I was going to say and how I was going to say it, when I was frustrated and angry with God because things were not working out the way I thought they should, when I was terrified of getting up in front of people and owning my Truth, when I was just in the part of the process that feels like crap—a friend, a messenger from God, told me a joke.

This joke is about a man who is talking to God, trying to understand God's perspective on things.

The man says to God, "What is a billion years like to you?"

God says, "A second."

And the man says, "Oh, that's interesting. Well, what is a billion dollars like to you?"

And God says, "A penny."

And the man, being human, of course starts calculating to himself, "Well, if a billion dollars is like a penny to God then a million must really be nothing. I'll bet I could get God to give me a million."

So the man says to God, "Can I have a million dollars?"

God says, "Sure... in a second."

God's time is perfect—it just doesn't feel like it to us all of the time. The more we can align our perspective with Truth the less we will feel like we are being punished.

By the way, the hardest part of unconditional Love is accepting wherever we are at in the moment no matter how uncomfortable. The hardest part of acceptance is not the difficulty of allowing others their process (although Lord knows that can be very hard); it is allowing ourselves our own process without shame and judgment.

I can do that now most of the time. I know now that when it feels like crap it is not punishment, it is not because I am bad or wrong or defective (although there is still a little part of me, that critical parent/disease voice that wants me to buy into that—and probably there always will be).

What I know now is that when it feels like shit that means that I am being fertilized to help me grow. I am so very grateful to God for all the wonderful fertilizer that has been poured on me over the years.

LOVE

The Universal Creative Force, as I understand it, is the energy field of ALL THAT IS vibrating at the frequency of Absolute Harmony. That vibrational frequency I call LOVE. (LOVE is the vibrational frequency of God; Love is an energy vibration within The Illusion which we can access; love is, in our Codependent culture, most often an addiction or an excuse for dysfunctional behavior.)

LOVE is the energy frequency of Absolute Harmony because it is the vibrational frequency where there is no separation.

Energy moves in wave-like patterns; what enables movement is the separation between the valley of the wave and its peak. The distance from peak to peak is called it's wavelength. It is a law of physics that as vibrational frequency rises, as it gets higher, the wavelength gets shorter.

125

The frequency of LOVE is the vibrational frequency where wavelength disappears, where separation disappears.

It is a place of absolute Peace, motionless, timeless, completely at rest: The Eternal Now.

The Peace and Bliss of The Eternal Now is the True Absolute Reality of the God-Force.

The illusion of separation—the distance, the separation, between the peak and the valley—is what makes motion possible. Separation is necessary for energy to be in motion. The illusion of separation was necessary to create The Illusion.

As part of the ONENESS of ALL THAT IS, we are God and God is LOVE. We are part of the Truth of ONENESS vibrating at the frequency of LOVE. As part of the ONENESS of LOVE we would *never* have been able to experience Love. It is kind of like, "If you are sugar then you never get to taste sugar."

In God we are LOVE. Without the illusion of separation we would never have had the opportunity to experience Love. Would never have been able to Love and be Loved.

Separation was necessary to allow us the incredible gift of experiencing Love, of Loving and being Loved.

The Illusion that caused all of the pain is also the vehicle for allowing us to feel and be Loved.

If you pursue your path of healing, I think that you will find as I have that it is very much worth it. It is worth it to be able to experience Love.

This is the Age of Healing and Joy. It is time to start remembering who you Truly are, to start feeling and tuning into the Truth which exists within you.

We are all butterflies.

We are all swans.

We are Spiritual Beings.

The Springtime of the Spirit has arrived: It is possible to learn to Love yourself.

It is possible to be happy, Joyous, and free—if you are willing to be scared and hurt, angry and sad.

You are Lovable.

You are Loved.

You are LOVE.

Joy to You & Me Enterprises

Robert Burney has formed Joy to You & Me Enterprises in order to facilitate the dissemination of what he believes is a vitally important and very Joyous message.

Codependence/The Dance of Wounded Souls is the first project for this company. At this time he is in the process of writing six more books which will follow this initial effort. Two of these books will be "how to" Recovery books—process level books dealing with the tools, dynamics, and principles of the Recovery process. The next three books will be *The Dance of the Wounded Souls Trilogy* which is written as an adult fable dealing with the mystical and metaphysical aspects of his message—including a History of the Universe unlike any ever written. The first book in this trilogy *Book 1—The Unicorn* is completed but will not be published until after the process level books. More will be revealed about the seventh book later.

Copies of *Codependence/The Dance of Wounded Souls* are available from Joy to You & Me Enterprises for $14.95 plus $3 for shipping and handling.

A four-hour audio tape set of the talk, "*Codependence/The Dance of Wounded Souls*" (this is 98% a literal recording of the book) is available for $19.95 plus $3 for shipping and handling.

The bumper sticker which is referred to in the book: "Work for World Peace—Heal Your Inner Child" is available for $3.50.

Please add 7.25% sales tax for books shipped to California addresses.

Information about Mr. Burney's availability for speaking and seminars can also be obtained by contacting:

Joy to You & Me Enterprises
Post Office Box 977
Cambria, California 93428